THE FIVE WORDS

Walking the healing path
through extreme emotions to fulfillment

M. KATHERINE MITCHELL, M.M.Q.

BALBOA.
PRESS

A DIVISION OF HAY HOUSE

Balboa Press books may be ordered through booksellers or by contacting:

Balboa Press
A Division of Hay House
1663 Liberty Drive
Bloomington, IN 47403
www.balboapress.com
1 (877) 407-4847

Because of the dynamic nature of the Internet, any web addresses or links contained in this book may have changed since publication and may no longer be valid. The views expressed in this work are solely those of the author and do not necessarily reflect the views of the publisher, and the publisher hereby disclaims any responsibility for them.

The author of this book does not dispense medical advice or prescribe the use of any technique as a form of treatment for physical, emotional, or medical problems without the advice of a physician, either directly or indirectly. The intent of the author is only to offer information of a general nature to help you in your quest for emotional and spiritual well-being. In the event you use any of the information in this book for yourself, which is your constitutional right, the author and the publisher assume no responsibility for your actions.

Any people depicted in stock imagery provided by Thinkstock are models, and such images are being used for illustrative purposes only.
Certain stock imagery © Thinkstock.

Print information available on the last page.

ISBN: 978-1-5043-8179-6 (sc)
ISBN: 978-1-5043-8181-9 (hc)
ISBN: 978-1-5043-8180-2 (e)

Library of Congress Control Number: 2017908638

Balboa Press rev. date: 08/18/2017

Dedication

The Five Words was written for anyone who struggles to understand their purpose, passion, and the sometimes overwhelming emotions that obscure that understanding. It is also for my family by blood or love who believe in me. They are my joy.

Contents

Preface and Acknowledgement

My exploration of Eastern medicine began in a class where I was introduced to the five element theory described in Traditional Chinese Medicine (TCM). Later, during our years of training in medical qigong my son-in-law, Michael Torok, and I spent a great deal of time discussing philosophy and exploring the edges of experience. At one of these *qications,* as we liked to call them, we discussed how the journey of the soul could be explained and explored with just a few words. When we studied the five element theory in depth during medical qigong classes, I remembered our discussion about the journey of the soul.

Naturally, between qications we were expected to practice what we had learned in class. As I practiced, I began making connections. The words Michael and I had come up with during our discussion of the soul correlated with the elements we learned about in five element theory. As it turns out, each word coincides nicely with one of the elements. The connection was astounding and thus *the Five Words* was born.

During this time I also realized that each of the five elements is described, in part, using archetypes. Archetypes are subtle energies that are woven into our lives and are the teaching formula we use for life lessons. This led me to Carolyn Myss and some of my even earlier studies of her work on archetypes. Her work expands and explains much about our relationship to emotions and their potential. Indeed, archetypes influence us all. As a result, archetypes became an important part of this discussion.

Since those early days, I completed my master training in medical qigong and have worked with people struggling with emotional crisis. Dealing with the big emotions is overwhelming for many people. As I thought more and more about that handful of words I came to believe that, with the help of the other disciplines mentioned, my five words would make the difficult understandable and life abound with possibility.

Throughout the years I have had many teachers and am grateful to them all. Special thanks to Katye and Alan Clark from Pennsylvania School of Spiritual Healing, Ted O'Brien of East Coast Institute of Medical QiGong, and Deborah and Jimmy Wray of Gateway School of Shamanism.

My best teachers and most loyal fans are, of course, my family. I owe extra thanks to my daughter Anastasia Torok, for her special gift as editor-in-chief. She had to remind me how to write and never lost faith that I could. I am eternally grateful to and for Michael Torok. His energy and enthusiasm is legendary. We teach each other. My husband, Howard, has shown the same unfailing belief in me as always and he has continued to support me throughout this project. I am also grateful to Eliese Zawacki for her technical support, honest insight, sweet perspective, loyalty, and encouragement. Finally, I am grateful to Jessica Mitchell for making so much of the journey with me and for pushing me to places I thought I could not reach both in life and in writing about *the Five Words*.

Chapter 1

Orientation

Five Words

Embracing the truth behind just five words enables you to create the life you want. The *Five Words* are: *choice, empowerment, commitment, boundaries, and compassion.* These are words common in our language but an understanding of their relevance to emotional balance, health, and fulfillment of life goals is largely missing. *The Five Words* will change that. You will learn to combat confusing life signals with ancient wisdom, science, direct experience, and a better understanding of these *Five Words.*

While throughout *the Five Words* I use examples and stories to explain certain realities, there is one important note that I must mention. Many questions need to be asked. The question, "Why?" is not one of them. "Why has this happened to me?" "Why am I going through this?" The truth is, knowing why rarely lends any solace, comfort, or healing. Usually knowing why just manages to complicate things by embroiling you in the emotions of the original incident and re-imprinting the trauma. Additionally, "Why me?" is the question of a victim, not an empowered person. If "Why?" is not the question, what is?

You need answers to questions like:

* "How do I feel about my current situation?"
* "What can I do about the emotions and energies in the situation?"
* "What can I understand and learn about myself in relation to what is going on?"
* "What is the best, most life-supporting action I can take now?"

Primal or Extreme Emotion

Each of the five words corresponds to a primal or extreme emotion. Emotional energies tend to make life feel chaotic or fragmented. With time and practice, however, you can work with these emotions to develop more coherent, constructive energies. It is not unusual to deny extreme emotions until you look at the masquerading or lesser emotions. For example, you may think you are not angry, but you do recognize feeling resentful or jealous. These are the masquerading or lesser emotions associated with the extreme emotion you know as anger. The following table lists the five extreme emotions and examples of their masquerading or lesser emotions. The chapters mentioned in the parenthesis are where you will find suggestions on working with these difficult emotions.

Extreme Emotion	Masquerading or Lesser Emotion
Fear (Chapter 3)	Rejection, insecurity, submissiveness, humiliation, worthlessness, or indecisiveness
Grief (Chapter 4)	Remorse, loneliness, boredom, apathy, alienation, vulnerability, abandonment, or guilt
Worry (Chapter 5)	Regrets, reminiscence, self-doubt, neediness, self-sacrifice, or rejection of attention
Shock (Chapter 6)	Anxiety, excitement, nervousness, confusion, mania, ecstasy, or eagerness
Anger (Chapter 7)	Resentment, rage, jealousy, irritability, frustration, judgment, depression, hurt, or hate

Five Element Theory

The Five Words is a blending of insights and learning from many sources. They encompass and summarize the journey of the soul. Mastery takes you from a state of high emotion to a state of knowing how to respond to the challenges you face on your way to fulfillment. Interestingly, these words reflect perfectly elements of Traditional Chinese Medicine (TCM) and, specifically, the five element theory. The following chapters tackle each of the five words, along with their corresponding element: water, metal, earth, fire, and wood.

As you journey through the work, you will explore extreme emotions and what it takes to embrace them. Once you realize how thoughts, feelings, and external events impact your well-being, you will begin to understand how emotion can cause changes to the physical body. Extreme emotions can, and do, change the physical body causing illness and disease. The Chinese have studied this for over five thousand years. They have amassed a body of knowledge and understanding that helps us appreciate what happens when extreme emotions are experienced again and again.

Over time, the Chinese ascertained which organ system is most provoked by which extreme emotion. This was accomplished through extensive study on how each emotion creates a response in the body. We now know the physical consequence of a heightened emotional state is chemical. Initially, the chemical response your body makes to an emotion slows or excites the energies depending on the situation. At first these responses don't do much lasting harm. If repeated often enough, however, the responses form stress, stress forms blocks, weaknesses, or constrictions, which ultimately manifest as disease in the body.

Archetypes

Understanding archetypes gives additional insight into how you can heal using the *Five Words*. Archetypes are energies. Like emotions, they are neither good nor bad. They are recognizable, describable energies that organize patterns of human behavior. Every archetype has a positive or light side potential and a challenging or dark side potential. Carl Jung spoke about archetypes in his early psychological works. Carolyn Myss has taken understanding of archetypes and their energies to a whole new level in her book *Sacred Contracts*.[1] According to Myss, we all have a core group of twelve archetypes that we bring into this life. Eight of these archetypes are unique to the individual, but four of them are part of everyone's makeup. The child, prostitute, saboteur, and victim archetypes are the four

---

[1] Carolyn Myss, *Sacred Contracts: awakening your divine potential*, (New York, Harmony Books, 2001).

we all have in common. These are what Myss calls your survival archetypes. Following is a summary of these survival archetypes.

The Child – Guardian of Innocence

The child archetype isn't so much about whether or not you act childish as it is about how playful you are or how quick you are to trust. This archetypal energy helps you decide when to be responsible or when to relax and depend on someone else. The child archetype is divided into several sub-archetypes such as: wounded child, magical child, divine child, nature child, or eternal child, among others. Each one carries energies in a particular pattern depending on the lessons chosen to work on in an incarnation. The sub-archetypes describe the energetic responses your so called inner child is likely to have during your life. For example, the wounded child looks at the world as hostile while the magical child tends to experience wonder and enchantment.

The Prostitute – Guardian of Faith

Yes. Everyone has a prostitute archetype. The prostitute may or may not have to do with sex. This archetypal energy is at play when you sell or negotiate away your body, mind, integrity, or spirit in exchange for security, safety, or personal gain. Prostitute energy expresses itself through an inability to divorce an abusive spouse or quit a job that is draining you. Fear (for survival, of change, of self-empowerment, *etc.*) is the hallmark of this archetype. When you finally decide the trade-off is insufficient, you can, and will, do what is necessary for yourself without compromising your integrity. Once you are able to abandon the impulse to prostitute yourself and you can embrace the truth of your abilities, this archetype surrounds you energetically with a *not for sale* sign. You gain a deep knowing that

5

your survival is possible without having to sacrifice the power of your spirit.

The Saboteur – Guardian of Choice

It has often been said that we are our own worst enemies. This is the consequence of saboteur energy. This energy is recognizable from the repetitious thoughts that are like recordings playing in your mind. These recordings convince you that you are not good enough, that you are not equipped to accomplish anything in life. The voice of this recording is you undermining yourself. It comes from patterns of thought and behavior that have accumulated over your lifetime. You have decided to believe in them, whether or not they are true. The saboteur induces self-destructive behavior with these thoughts and wreaks havoc in your life.

Getting in your own way can be as simple as consistently being late to appointments but it can be complicated as well. If you feel sure you cannot find (or don't deserve) a better partner and, as a result, you stay in an abusive relationship, you are listening to your archetypal saboteur. This energy can also cause you to undermine others. When the saboteur becomes your ally and you start operating from the light side of the archetype, you understand when you are about to sabotage yourself or others in time to prevent the destructive impulse.

The Victim – Guardian of Self-Esteem

Everyone has seen news reports of people experiencing real and intentional horrors. Once the horror is over, however, a person's response to having been victimized tells the story of the light or shadow aspects of the victim archetype. A person working in the energies of the shadow victim archetype always feels taken advantage of and never takes responsibility for whatever happens.

Once you make the victim energies your ally, these destructive energies fall away.

As a community we have devised support groups for victims and these can be helpful. Sometimes, however, a person continues to play the victim for sympathy, attention, and positive feedback. Indeed, some people find real currency in their wounds. Mastery of the victim archetype allows you to recognize when you are in danger of being victimized, either through passivity or inappropriate actions. It also provides some clarity concerning whether or not you are about to victimize someone else. Insight and clarity are important gifts.

Dr. Stephen Karpman described the victim triangle as a model of human interaction in his 1968 article, Fairy tales and script drama analysis.[2] Essentially this model describes how the victim, perpetrator, and rescuer archetypes interact. A perpetrator, by his or her actions, creates a victim. A rescuer comes to aid the victim. Sooner or later the victim resents or rejects the rescuer and thereby makes the rescuer feel like a victim. The perpetrator can now step into the rescuer's role. Everyone changes roles. The former victim is now the perpetrator; the former rescuer is now the victim, making room for the old perpetrator to become the new rescuer. Entering into the victim triangle on any level ensures that you will eventually play all three roles.

Interaction of the Four Survival Archetypes

How do these archetypes play out in you? All children are vulnerable and sensitive to the whims of others. Depending on how a child is treated he or she can grow up to be optimistic and hopeful or confused and anxious. Children are often cautioned not to try something because it's too dangerous. A child might hear,

[2] Karpman, S. (1968). Fairy tales and script drama analysis. Transactional Analysis Bulletin, 7(26), 39-43.

"Be careful, you'll fall!" or, "You are going to cut yourself!" for example, and this causes uncertainty and fear reactions. The child infers that there is something wrong with him or her that makes it impossible to accomplish what is desired. The childhood myth, *I'm not good enough*, sets up conditions for saboteur energy to manifest in the adult. A child is also very quick to learn how to sublimate his or her own will in order to win approval. This behavior activates the prostitute as well as the victim archetypes when taken into adulthood.

Survival archetypes come into play in all areas of your life. Besides the survival archetypes there are eight other archetypes that make up your core group of helper energies. Each of the five elements also has a governing archetype that will aid you in your work toward soul fulfillment. These will be explained in the chapter that discusses the element with which the archetype is associated.

Tying It Together

Extreme Emotion	Masquerading Emotions	TCM Element	Governing Archetype	Word	Coherent Emotions
Fear (Chapter 3)	Loneliness Insecurity Alienation Worthlessness Inferiority Shame	Water	Sage	Choice	Faith Wisdom Confidence Awe Inner-strength Perseverance
Grief (Chapter 4)	Remorse Loneliness Boredom Judgmental Apathy Vulnerability Abandoned Emptiness Guilt	Metal	Alchemist	Empowerment	Integrity Reverence Dignity Respect Acceptance Dependability Inspiration Appreciation Endurance
Worry (Chapter 5)	Regretful Reminiscent Self-doubting Needy Self-sacrificing Self-absorbed Dread	Earth	Mother	Commitment	Trust Openness Empathy Feeling safe Nourished Altruism Service
Shock (Chapter 6)	Anxiety Excitement Nervousness Confusion Mania Ecstatic Dismay Insomnia Astonished Excessive Joy Coldness	Fire	Lover and Protector	Boundaries	Open-hearted Peaceful Content Joyful Intimacy Tranquility Expressiveness Activated Expansive Optimistic Hopeful
Anger (Chapter 7)	Resentment Depression Jealousy Irritability Frustration Judgmental Hateful Defensive Insecure	Wood	Warrior and Visionary	Compassion	Acceptance Forgiving Empathic Kind Understanding Self-assertive Able to Respond

A Few Words about Words

Good/bad, light/dark, bright/shadow; these opposites expose an essential mistake we all make. Society assigns emotional qualities and value judgments to them. The truth is, these opposites generate perspective, equal in their ability to teach, to sustain, and to create your world. The light side of your personality is just what society determines is good. The same is true for your dark side which society considers bad. In different context, the good or bad of the situation may be very different. In other words, there is no good or bad. What really is true? Opposites present an opportunity to expand understanding and grow spiritually by examining and owning all sides of the picture.

Words are powerful tools. They will encourage you or defeat you. Words are capable of healing or destroying you. This is especially true of your own words. No words have more consequence, for good or ill, than those you say to yourself.

Journaling

Soul healing and growth requires a tool for reflection. The best tool is a journal. A journal has the potential to be your own best friend. Your journal is the place where your words, private thoughts, and experiences can be safely recorded and reflected upon. It is a tool that allows the whole scope of your personal experience a venue for expression. Once started, a journal can provide the stepping stones that open up memories and possibilities that you have forgotten. It is a place where you can be honest, even if the truth is not flattering. No one is without a shadow side. No one is all good or all bad. Only by acknowledging both your light *and* dark sides can you become whole and heal.

It is important to realize that you don't have to write volumes. In fact, doing so is what stops the journaling process for many of us. Beginners often write page after page. It soon becomes too much and journaling ends. There seems to be the expectation that all of your entries must rival that original grand effort. This is not true. Be succinct and regular in your journal entries. Even short entries will help you see patterns, problems, and processes more easily.

Asking Questions

In order to facilitate working with each of the *Five Words*, I have included a section called *Questions for Your Journal* after each chapter. Some of these questions can be quite lengthy to answer. Do it at your pace and record the answers in your journal. There is no right or wrong answer to the questions. They are an opportunity to think about your life in the context of the *Five Words*. The answers to the questions will help you appreciate where your actual approach to life comes from and what needs to change. They are a jumping off point for your personal journey toward a better understanding of you!

Chapter 2

The Journey Begins

As a child, I had a favorite doll. This doll was not so different from my other baby dolls except that it was black skinned and I am not. My love for this particular doll distressed someone in my family. After a day of loving and tending my special doll, I would tuck her into the bed I made for her so that I would be sure to know exactly where she was the next morning. Always, when I woke up, my baby doll was gone. Eventually, my mother would find her again and I would spend one more day tending her with love and special care. Again, I would tuck her into bed in the perfect spot I made for her and again, the next day, she would be gone. It happened repeatedly. I was frantic each time trying to find my baby doll. Finally, mom just didn't find her again.

Many years later, I was at a class where information about past lives often came out. I was told about one of my past lives in Africa. Slavers came and either murdered or kidnapped everyone in my village for the slave trade. I survived to watch as my husband was killed and my child taken. At the time, there was nothing I could do about any of it. Upon hearing this in class, I felt all of the air leave my body. I felt as if my soul collapsed. My body caved in; I wanted to curl into my great nightmare. I knew this story was true to the very depths of my being. Every cell in my body screamed and cried for the losses I suffered in that lifetime. I felt it as if it were just happening: fresh and real and devastating. Later, I remembered my baby doll. She was an artifact of that life bleeding through into this one.

This is an example of cellular memory. Cellular memory is not conscious, but it is perhaps more powerful because of its subconscious nature. It is possible in that lifetime I could have run out to fight for my family; I don't know what stopped me. Had I done so, I most assuredly would have been taken or killed. Instead, I lived with regret, shame, self-loathing, shock, rejection, guilt, rage, grief, and fear for the rest of that lifetime; and I carried it forward with me into this life. In this lifetime, without conscious memory of that one, every decision seemed too big to make, what would people think if they actually knew the truth about me? What if they knew that I had failed? I felt I didn't deserve any kindness. I couldn't be seen. I must hide. Because of that lifetime, and without consciously understanding why, everything now seemed to be life or death. That life I felt I had lost everything and there was no hope. In this life, every choice was between loss and hopeless.

After recalling that life experience, I was prompted to journey into understanding and embracing the power of emotion, history, myth, and what became a specific set of *Five Words*. It is my hope that in exploring this story, and others, you will to come to understand the gift of your powerful emotions and recognize a path to a fuller expression of your soul's agenda.

A very wise man once said, "Carnation is enough." It is not necessary to believe in reincarnation to see the effects of cellular memory. For example: adults with no memory of sexual abuse as children find themselves reliving the experience, or soldiers coming back from war can suddenly be back in the jungle fighting for their lives. Profound memories, even though buried, can be triggered. The trigger can be anything: a smell, a taste, a sound, how material moves in particular lighting. Experiences like this are real and have a huge impact on the people experiencing them. They are emotionally charged and riveting. They require attention. Sometimes that means counseling or outside help. It always means acknowledging these emotions and healing through your own conscious work.

Even without traumatic events in life, everyone has emotions. No matter how or when they come to us, emotions are a part of everyone's life. Extreme emotions, the really big ones, are often denied and repressed, especially anger and fear. Those people, who profess to feel nothing, do still have emotions. Emotions are how you know you are alive and what sometimes cause you to wish otherwise. They are the evidence of your experience and the catalysts of change. They define the conditions of your life and they are your means of growth toward fullness of spirit and fullness of life.

Learning what your emotions are, what to do with them, how they matter, and what they can teach you is pretty much what the journey of life on this planet is about. Do you manage your emotions or do they manage you? Do emotions lead you to heights of glory or depths of madness? Are they the keys to the kingdom of spiritual growth and freedom, or the clang of the prison door? Or, are emotions all of the above?

It is helpful to think of emotion as an ocean. In the middle of this ocean sits a boat comprised of all the baggage, experience, and reactions you have used to make up your life story. On a clear day the water is calm, breezes refresh and revitalize you, birds call and small clouds scuttle above. Other days the ocean is rough. Waves crash into the boat, sometimes over it. The wind howls and birds have long since flown to sanctuary. The storm literally rocks your world. Your very existence is challenged on precarious seas.

What can you do? You can do things that create stability in your craft. You can ride it out or you can move to a place of safety. Sometimes you feel over-whelmed, too tired, or convinced you are not skilled enough to handle your situation. You may feel hopeless or helpless. You may feel that the storm is bigger than you are, more powerful than you. You may give up; leave the wheel hoping that someone else will guide the boat to safety. You may run below to put on a life jacket. You may shout to the heavens that this part of the journey is not your responsibility, that you cannot do this.

The ocean, however, is as much a part of the landscape of your life as the boat! How do you change the ocean? Perhaps the secret is to learn strategies to deal with the ocean, gaining understanding of the cycles and currents, fortify against the storm, prepare, and practice. This is what brings you through to the other side of the storm stronger.

Like the ocean, emotions can present powerful challenges in life and, like the ocean, emotions are neutral. The ocean is neither good nor bad. Even the really big emotions are compliments and color points on a scale of light and shadow that describe life. Emotions are neither good nor bad. Emotions simply are. They are fluid and vary in intensity and duration.

In Traditional Chinese Medicine (TCM) yin and yang are, in part, an expression of the extremes of creation and the continual movement that maintains balance. In the same way, yin and yang express emotion. For example, grief is a yin emotion and anger is yang. Other yin aspects of creation include the moon, shade, the stagnant, cool, calm, and restful while yang is characterized by the sun, bright, warming, explosive, vital, and active. All levels of emotion are some combination of yin and yang as is the ocean itself, moving and vital, quiet and deep.

Emotions are the gifts of Creator God that give us the opportunity to experience life. They are cyclical, sometimes surging and grasping like a riptide. They come in waves, sometimes supporting and uplifting and sometimes, like the perfect storm, threatening to engulf and destroy. Fortunately, you can begin to understand, fortify, prepare, and practice.

All emotions are sourced in love, the great creative life force that is God. Love is not an extreme emotion; it is the original state of being. It is the impulse of creation. Gradually, as love expressed into light and shadow, yin and yang, all of creation came into being, as did the whole range of emotion. In God there is only love, all light and shadow *is* the love of God expressing and teaching. There is no intention from God for the soul to experience suffering. On earth, however, we have stepped beyond the understanding of what is true. Instead we struggle with what we have created from what is true and suffering happens. Free will allows us to manipulate this beautiful creation and we do not always act in love. We have created the energies that compromise Eden. Our work on the planet is to bring those energies back into balance, back to that original state of being: love.

By understanding where your journey starts, you can begin the work of bringing yourself back into balance. Before birth, you make binding soul agreements to set up conditions for the experiences you wish to have while on earth. Agreements are made in order to populate your life with the cast of characters needed to experience your lesson plan. These agreements, or sacred contracts, may be for a short time or a life time. That is to say, they include everyone from the person you see for only moments whose smile encourages you, to your friends, your boss, and the people of your family. These agreements are made from the level of love only, purely love. All parties agree to the plan.

It is true that the people who seem to give you your hardest lessons on earth are those that love you most on the level of soul. Sacred contracts constitute the lessons you have decided to take on in order to learn and, thereby, change the energies you created in less enlightened times. There are no bad guys here. There are only people who love you enough to show up in your life in a way that allows you to learn and grow according to your plan.

When you are born... you forget the plan.

How Did You Get Here?

Tribe and Personal Myths

Everyone has a tribe. Parents, teachers, church leaders, peers, *etc.* constitute your tribe. You arrive as an infant fresh and bright with promise. At first, you cannot do much of anything wrong, but as you grow things seem to change. Your tribe teaches you early in life that you are expected to understand your place and behave in a prescribed way. Members of your tribe mean well, or at least they are doing the best they can to give you everything they believe you need. Remember, each of these people has been influenced by their own tribes and experience. Under the tutelage of your tribe, your experience begins to teach you where you are safe, what can be done, who can be trusted, and what is expected.

A baby in the womb or sleeping in its mother's arms is absorbing the thoughts, emotions, attitudes, and energies of everything and everyone that comes in contact with him or her. This baby is already assimilating the energies of the tribe. Absorbing is automatic. Energies are felt on all levels: physical, mental, emotional, and spiritual. A baby has an unfiltered ability to pick up on all of these cues and has little ability to filter for appropriateness or validity.

Sensing is a child's ability to learn by feeling the surrounding energies. It is the most powerful survival tool in use during the formative years. Information is inferred, witnessed, spoken, demonstrated, or felt. Sense ability may be blunted as birthdays come and go by people who repudiate what they see as childish perceptions. Once you are twelve years old you are pretty well programed to believe what the tribe believes, whether it is ultimately true and right for you or not.

Your tribe is made up of people who carefully teach you what to think. Your own thought processes are neither encouraged nor validated, as a rule. Around age eight, peers begin to play a big role in your identity. You find you need to belong, to be liked. You try to fit in, never realizing your peers have tribes that have molded and conditioned them, which means you now have that tribe's dynamic to assimilate. Eventually, you decide which part of you needs to be hidden, which needs to be denied or pushed away, and exactly what needs to be polished up to make you appear at your best.

Added to this development is media influence. Public media is not necessarily an obvious member of your tribe. Still, things like magazines, television, movies, and gaming platforms, give you models or heroes that tell you how to look, how to act, what is acceptable, what is ugly, what should be rejected, *etc.*. The media presents their version of the perfect man or woman. By the time you become a teenager, you feel you must look like a model and act like a superhero! When you decide you don't measure up, you feel unworthy, ugly, or maybe weak, *etc.* It depends on which model you buy into.

Most of us believe we have failed to meet the expectations we inherited from our tribe. On a personal level this means you believe you are far from perfect but you honestly believe others are very close. You tend to be generous with excuses for other people's failings but you are heartless toward yourself.

From this you create your own myth. A myth is a fiction you create that tells the story of your insufficiency, imperfection, or lack when compared to others. Myths also tell the other side of the story about feelings of superiority and entitlement. These personal myths are not necessarily accurate nor kind, but you believe them to be true. You combine all of the information gathered in your lifetime with a child's belief that it must be true because you have been told so for as long as you can remember. A myth speaks of your insecurities.

A myth of inadequacy or superiority throws your reality out of balance and blocks your ability to be in the world as it is. Myths inhibit your ability to act appropriately in situations that arise. Many of us struggle daily with how to be a better person and make a bigger difference. Some people are actually starting to turn away from the messages they have been spoon-fed since they were tiny. Unfortunately, all too often those myths are replaced with similar fear-based myths sourced from the same set of misinformed places. Some of us have tried to stop feeling altogether through will or medication. Fear, mistrust, addiction, and the thoughts you think about yourself become part of your personal myth.

Suddenly, all of your childhood potential and promise seem lackluster. You look down on yourself, perhaps secretly, but look up to other people who seem to have it all, whose life seems easy. You feel you should be doing more, making a bigger difference, you should be better. What you don't realize is that the people you are looking up to also often have hidden beliefs that they are not doing enough, they are not good enough, they will never be enough, and they must hide that desperate, dirty secret from everyone.

What are your myths? How do you get at the truth behind your personal myths? What is it that you actually believe about yourself, your family, your country, and the world? It is relatively simple to discover the nature of the myths you have adopted. To do so you must listen. Listen to how you talk to yourself. Is your self-talk, "I never get a break," or, "This is what always happens to me," when something doesn't go your way? When you want to interact with people do you think, "I have nothing interesting to say," "These people are beneath me," "I'm too shy," "I can't talk to anyone," "I always make a fool out of myself," or "I can't dance, (cook, play games, *etc.*")?

Myths expand to contaminate your attitudes about safety, conduct, desirability, and possibilities. Are you always some version of too fat, too thin, too tall, too short, too ugly, too stupid, too good, too important, too smart, too forgetful, too young, too old, too weak, or too uneducated, *etc.*? These thoughts are automatic responses that play in your head almost like a recording playing on repeat mode. All of these feelings, images, and self-messages are your myths. They are limiting beliefs you hold about yourself. These beliefs stifle your creative spark and potential.

Myths are what limit you. Myths come out as a voice in your head giving you messages about your worth. They are so well ingrained that most times you don't know they are not appropriate or true. Even when you start to question their validity, they cause problems; they are that automatic. For example, how often does, "Oh you idiot!" or "You clumsy oaf!" spring to mind when any little thing happens? The voice of the auto-response in your mind may or may not be your own, but the sentiment is one you have heard, or imagined, all of your life from members of your tribe.

Emotions and Energy

Whether acknowledged or not, emotions fuel everything you do, and attempts to control or manipulate them fail or backfire. There are people who do not believe they have emotions. They restrict all of the so called "bad" emotions through acts of their will; after all, a lady shouldn't get angry and a man doesn't cry. They repress, hide, and deny their emotions, but they still have them. Pharmaceuticals, alcohol, and recreational drug use can and do suppress or distort emotions: ALL emotions. Medications for depression also suppress joy. Emotions are there for you to *feel*. They are not something to run from, or from which to hide.

Life is essentially dual by nature. You have to experience contrast, the give and take, the ebb and flow. Without dark, you cannot know light; without sadness you cannot know joy. As a result, one of the great truths about emotion is you don't get to choose which emotions you feel. You can be open or closed to feeling, both is not possible. Again, if you suppress anger, you also suppress joy.

As quantum mechanics is teaching, when it comes right down

to it, *everything is energy!*[3] There is an energy vibration in everything, although the vibratory rate differs. Rocks vibrate slowly, plants more quickly, and animals faster yet. Differences in vibration can be observed: one person never seems to get tired, the next is always tired, one animal stays very still and another is moving almost constantly. What is right for one is not right for the other. A sloth must move slowly to manage life in its environment. A hawk swoops out of the sky to catch his food. Life expresses according to the lesson or need of the individual. No path or vibratory difference is inappropriate. Rocks, plants, animals, insects, and people vibrate at a specific and perfect level to express the individual.

Surrounding and permeating the physical body is your energy field, sometimes called an aura. The aura is made of the vibration of your physical body combined with the vibrations of subtle bodies. This combination makes up your energetic signature. Subtle bodies, from the densest vibration to the highest are: the emotional body, the mental body, the spiritual body, and the astral or etheric body. Each of these bodies vibrates at its own unique frequency and reflects perfectly the condition of the individual who generates them. In other words, your energy field is made up of the subtle aspects of the self that dances with the environment through the physical body.

Everything is energy. According to TCM and many other schools of thought, all parts of the universe are connected by this energy. Everything shares in the universal energy that some people call Divine and some call physics. The name isn't as important as the understanding of this basic idea. Everything has vibration or energy, including thoughts and emotion.

With muscle testing you can discover how thoughts impact your energy and strength. Find a friend and have them put their arm out. Ask them to resist your effort to push their arm down.

---

[3] http://www.collective-evolution.com/2014/09/27/this-is-the-world-of-quantum-physics-nothing-is-solid-and-everything-is-energy/

Push it down. This will show you how strong they are normally. Now silently direct this thought toward your friend, "You are such a weakling, you cannot do anything." Again ask them to resist you when you push down on their arm. You will find they are not as strong as they were the first time. Now fix it. Mentally think, "You are strong and competent in all you do." Check the arm strength again. It will be strong again. A negative thought will make a person physically weaker; a positive thought will make them stronger. The thoughts you direct toward yourself are even more damaging and can also be observed with this muscle testing experiment.

By seeing the results of muscle testing you can understand that there are real connections between the physical, social, mental, emotional, and spiritual aspects of daily life. You can understand, as the ancient Chinese did, how disruptive energy on one level can impact other levels. Major events, such as the Challenger space shuttle disaster or the terrorist attacks of September 11th, can change the consciousness and emotion of the entire world in one moment. As these events unfolded, everyone was affected in some way.

Continuing this idea, we are all affected by the thoughts, words, actions, and reactions of every other being on the planet at some level. It is not necessary to have a conscious knowledge of a situation to feel that something has happened. I was driving home one night after visiting my family in another town. When I crested the mountain and started to drive into the valley where I lived, I was overcome by great dread and then fatigue. A policeman pulled me over because I seemed to be driving erratically. He told me to be safe and let me go since he could see I was not intoxicated. I pulled myself together to continue the drive. The next day I learned that multiple sadistic murders had been committed the previous night in the valley into which I was driving. The energy created by these horrible murders is what I felt as I began my descent into the valley. The vibration or energy of everything that has happened stays around for all to experience on some level.

The Ego

The ego is that very small part of the self that imagines it is in charge. When the ego attaches to a particular emotion it can become habituated or addicted to it and can, thereby, become dependent on it for attention or justification. Some egos take it so far as to engage in what Carolyn Myss calls woundology. If you engage in woundology, you cling to an emotional trauma like a life raft or badge of courage and make it a permanent, and defended, part of your identity. This is behavior typical of the ego.

The ego creates itself with a few tools from you: imprints, old outdated beliefs, social patterns, and the personal myths you believe in. Imprints are big and little experiences that you may not remember but that still have an impact on your thoughts and actions. Cell memory is a big imprint. Outdated beliefs are made up of information that was good when it was learned but, for whatever reason, is no longer valid. A simple example of this would be a parent telling her child to always hold an adult's hand when crossing the street. This is good information for a three year old but is rather restrictive for an adult. Social patterns are beliefs learned from the tribe. These belief patterns form your *shoulds* which are the nagging expectations of behavior as in; *I should* do this or that.

You need to place control of your life back in the hands of your soul. The ego's job is to keep you safe. It is the front man for the soul/self that you really are. As you can guess, the tools ego uses to manage your life could come from better sources. Each of these tools has the capacity to disturb the vibratory rate of your body and cause blockages to form along the energetic pathways associated with the source emotion. The soul acts only from love.

Questions for Your Journal

- How kind is my self-talk?
- Can I consider the possibility that my attitudes of self-judgment such as "I am not enough" or "I am too good for this" are invalid?
- Investigating *Dis*empowerment: What are my core beliefs about myself? Where do the beliefs I have about my worth come from? If it is something I was told, how old do I feel when I hear this voice? Use the headings below to make your list. (This can be a very long list.)

<u>Core Belief</u>   <u>Origin of Belief</u>   <u>Age</u>

1.
2.
3.
Etc.

Beginning the Healing Path with the Five Words

You are repeatedly offered opportunities to learn the lessons you have planned for yourself. One such opportunity is not enough to upset the balance in the physical body necessarily, but you are given the lesson as many times as it takes to learn it. An example of this would be the woman who marries the same kind of man over and over again. When a hot-button issue comes up, that is, one where your reaction is out of proportion to the situation, you can be certain your overblown reaction is due to old unresolved experiences, imprints, outdated beliefs, and/or personal myths. Emotion from each past experience adds to the current experience and compounds the current reaction. Each repetition of the lesson disrupts the harmonious flow of energy and agitates or suppresses your energy field. The energy of the experience, if not resolved, is stored in the body and accumulates as congestion until it manifests as disease.

The Five Words, with the help of TCM and archetypes, will help you to recognize extreme emotions, imprints, outdated beliefs, and your personal myths. *The Five words* will show you how to take appropriate steps to reform your hot-button issues. TCM assigns the element and organ systems specific emotions. Body problems in these areas will give you a clue about which emotions to work on within the context of the Five Words. Archetypes describe the energies in play. On the light side of the archetype is a template for behavior that allows you to experience and release your extreme emotion, to float over the cresting crashing wave of experience. On the shadow side is a catalyst to encourage growth. Together, these tools will teach you how to grow into the person you were meant to be.

The Five Words teach you how to change your responses to life challenges for the betterment of health and a more balanced and progressive life. They will bring about realizations for the journey to emotional freedom and full expression of your true self. Using the Five Words takes brutal self-honesty; yet, there is no more important journey you can possibly take. Nothing is more vital than fulfilling your soul's plan and the brilliant promise with which you were born.

Chapter 3

First Word – Choice

*"Faith and Fear both demand you believe in
something you cannot see; you choose!"*

Bob Proctor, www.proctorgallagherinstitute.com

Extreme Emotion: Fear

TCM Element: Water Element

TCM Organ Systems/Meridians: Kidney/Bladder

Archetype: Sage, Guardian of Wisdom

Everything comes down to choice. Every infinitesimal moment of consciousness is imbued with the steering wheel of choice. The boat that is your life sinks, flounders, or floats on the ocean of emotion depending on choice. Emotions truly are just like water, calm and sweet, stormy and cold, deep or shallow. Water is patient, persistent, and flexible. It is powerful, and it is neutral. Like water, emotions, even fear, are neutral. How you *choose* to respond to your emotions dictates your experience with them.

Emotions are energy. Simply, they are catalysts of action. As has been stated, emotions are the means you have to know that something is changing or needs to be changed. They are psycho-physiological responses to situations in the environment that are meant to elicit action. Consider the surge of adrenalin when you are confronted by someone whom you know wants to harm you. You feel sudden fear. Because of the danger you must decide if you are going to turn and run, or hold your ground. This is the classical fight or flight response. Emotions are the tools that allow you to have meaningful experiences and interact with your environment. By giving you a deep awareness of your physical existence and experience, emotions alert you to the possibility of a choice point.

In some ways, choice is the most important of the five words. Perhaps this is because in every moment of every day, in times of action or inaction, choices are being made. It may not seem so, but it is assuredly true. Choose to clean your house or choose to play video games, choose to live in your wounds or to heal them, choose to be abused at work or to change it, choose to believe in goodness, or choose to see only hardship. The list goes on forever. Accepting ridicule is a choice; being constantly tired is a choice, being unwilling to see how your choices create fatigue is a choice; as is doing nothing about it. Every pound you wear, every pain you feel, every emotion that threatens to overcome you is a matter of choice *on some level*.

Ultimately, the choice is what will you do with the emotion? I am not suggesting that emotions should be suppressed; quite the contrary! Treat them like a fishing expedition: catch and release. Emotions need to be named, captured, observed, learned from, and finally released without prejudice.

What does it take to make a good choice? Even doing nothing and allowing things to continue as they are is a choice? Making no choice is, in fact, a choice. Why do nothing? Why make no decision? How can you be indecisive when your happiness is at stake? Sometimes indecisiveness is simply a matter of too many choices or unclear goals. In other cases, experience teaches us certain behaviors will lead to dire consequences. Many people have ample experience to understand this from their current lives. Historically, a slave who ran away was beaten or killed; a thief was sentenced to have his hand cut off; a healer was branded a witch and burned at the stake. Sometimes you just fear the unknown. It takes courage to choose.

It is important to realize that you are making choices all the time. There have been barbarous times in human history, and while you don't necessarily carry current memories from these experiences, the traditions of witch burning and the terror caused by slavers, the inquisition, and the holocaust, *etc.* are carried in your cells. You have some level of direct knowledge of these experiences as cellular memory. Your choices are made based on your current knowledge, experiences, fears, personal myths, and sometimes, things you just know from cellular memory. Your choices create your world.

Water Element

(Kidneys and Bladder)

"The mysterious powers of winter create the extreme cold in heaven and they create water upon the earth. Within the body they create the bones, and of the orifices they create the Kidneys. Of the colors they create the black color. They give to the human voice the ability to groan and to hum. In times of excitement and change they create trembling, and among the emotions they create fear."

Nei Ching

Water is the first element: essential, beautiful, and terrible water! You begin in water, you cannot live without it, yet it can easily destroy you. The emotional shadow of this element is fear in all its manifestations. Fear makes you cautious and inhibited, perhaps isolated, hyper-vigilant, and overly sensitive to stimulation. Other fear responses include loneliness and insecurity, indecisiveness, alienation, feelings of worthlessness, and inferiority, *etc*. On the light side, when you overcome fear you develop attributes like faith, wisdom, clear perception, self-confidence, awe, inner strength, perseverance, and trust. Fear and all of these water element responses will be addressed herein as fear.

The yin internal organ is the kidney, the yang organ is the bladder, the sense organs are the ears, and the tissue is the bones. TCM tells you that problems or disease in these organs or tissues can indicate a need to address the extreme emotion of fear. Traditionally the season associated with the water element is winter; the color is deep blue/black, and the sound is groaning. The color, sound, and purging tones are helpful in releasing and soothing the intensity of fear and its associated emotions.

For the rest of my life in Africa, and for most of this one, my life has been governed by fear. Other lives have added to that fear. It is a most basic fear: I am not safe. In this life, while my parents were screaming at each other, the other children strained at the door to catch every word. I cowered. I tried to hide. I couldn't stand to hear. The very people who were my source of protection were out of control. Nightmares were common and my sisters, saints that they were, tolerated me trying my best to sleep underneath them so I could hide. Eventually I stopped dreaming; but as I got older my waking life didn't feel much better. The insecurity was excruciating. As I grew up, depression, and indecisiveness became my mode of operation. I was just too afraid.

Every one of us has some history that has been retold or reinforced in some way throughout time and in this lifetime. Every time my baby doll was gone, my fear was subtly reinforced. The actions of my tribe in this life unwittingly echoed my experience and re-impressed on my subconscious mind that I was not safe here.

Fear is the means of your great *dis*empowerment! Fear feeds and fuels every extreme emotion you have. You lose perspective;

you cannot adapt. It is easy to become overwhelmed and exhausted. The waves of fear increase and intensify with worry. Fear fuels and aggravates anger and depression. Only when you choose to go into the depths of yourself can you find the great stillness that is deep water. From there you find faith to calm the waves of your emotions.

Faith, like still deep water, is pure potential. Water is patient, persistent and flexible. This is the power of the water element. It is tenacious; it can be diverted, but not stopped as it travels toward the sea. Water wears down obstacles in its path and creates something different as it passes. Faith also diminishes obstacles. Faith reinforces wisdom; wisdom builds self-confidence, and perspective. Faith allows you to be positive about your ability to pursue your life dreams. Faith allows you to persevere with will and intelligence, and adapt to changes in your situation. Faith is a choice and a position of strength from which all things are possible.

Faith or fear, you have a choice. That is not to say that the choice is easy, but it is simple.

Fear is the ego distracting you. The ego's job is to protect, define and perhaps justify the personality. The personality is just the window dressing the soul wears in this lifetime. Ego traps you in fear built from past experiences which it projects onto the future. The ego is willing and able to create a habit of fear and mechanisms to empower fear.

Faith is the choice you make to proclaim that you will live *now.* The past is gone, the future is not here. Now is the only time you have available to affect your life. Now is your only point of power. Living in the present moment, learn from the past and make plans for the future. Do not go to either place to live as fear would have you do. Honor the lessons of the past but don't dwell on them and thereby magnify their importance. Make plans for the future without becoming too attached to those plans. Things change. Faith allows you to stay flexible, like water, and move with each moment.

Now you are in position to truly respect yourself and your journey. You are in a position to live fully rather than hiding for fear something may go wrong. You can be strong where you need to be, flow around obstacles, even change course, when that is required. Most importantly, you can choose how to *act* rather than just react. Choices can be made with will and wisdom from a foundation of trust and with awareness of what is true and right for you. You live in empowered balance. The choice is to drown in fear or use your faith, will power, and personal wisdom to travel through life.

It is necessary to examine the choices you make. Many choices are automatic and don't require a great deal of thought. These choices, however, need to be reconsidered. What is easy or what has always been done is not necessarily the right thing for your growth or the essential expression of your soul. The same old response may not be serving you well.

Making good choices require that you look to your value system, your standard of integrity, and your personal spiritual goals. You fear making the wrong choice. Have faith and choose. This is the most selfless thing a person can do. Only from a position of honest self-direction can your choices give to you and to others in any powerful way. Your gift to humanity is unique; it is yours to define through your choices. Those choices are most powerful when not diluted or complicated by fear.

Remember, fear creates disempowerment and is exhausting. Fear makes your life too busy. You try to hide from what makes you uncomfortable, as do we all. You are overscheduled and overworked out of fear. Fear, with the help of ego, creates a habit of busy. It creates the keep up with the Jones; get it done or lose your job; and you're not good enough myths. Choice makes room for you to express who you really are and faith enables that choice.

Water Element Archetype

SAGE: Guardian of Wisdom

Understanding the scope of the Sage archetype will help define the energies and impulses the Water Element brings into your life. Sage is teacher, shaman, mentor, wizard, and guide. Like the water element, the Sage finds a patient way through, around, and/or beyond obstacles. Water finds its level and simply continues. That is wisdom.

The wise one sees every choice point and makes a patient way through. The possibilities are endless. Choice is powerful, flexible, and unstoppable like water. The Sage, also powerful, flexible, and unstoppable, makes a choice to maintain a level bearing against fear, holds onto the rudder in the storm, and guides his boat of life to fulfillment of his soul's plan.

What Can I Do?

The lessons of the sage archetype and the water element encourage you to practice *self-care*. Self-care is so important it is recommended after every one of the five words and has its own chapter (chapter 8). Self-care is especially important for your water element responses. As I have said, fear is a factor in all of your extreme emotions. To take care of yourself, you must specifically:

- Be your first priority! This quiet self-care is important to calm the chaotic voice of fear.
- Make your down-time count. Do something that will build your confidence and joy in the world. What are you good at? What do you love?
- Be mindful of your need to be by yourself; it is how you find out who you are and what you want.

Indulge in the luxury of quiet. A mind full of continuous chatter is a distraction and disperses your energy. Be mindful of your thoughts. During the muscle testing exercise you saw that thoughts are powerful. If your thoughts are running away with your quietude, sing a song or listen to a guided meditation.

In meditation, or before falling asleep, breathe in the color of the water element. This is a deep blue/black like the depths of the ocean. Imagine that you breathe the color into your kidneys and then exhale any expressions of fear or insecurity you feel in your body. Every emotion has a corresponding physical sensation. You can exhale through these physical sensations as if you are washing them from your body. Allow your body to relax into the depths of the color.

Wear water element colors. Consciously imagine the depths of the ocean surrounding and protecting you. Wearing water element colored clothing is almost common these days and is passed off as business attire. This says a lot about the hostility and fear in the business world.

Be mindful of what you put in your body. Drugs, alcohol, caffeine, and highly processed or sweetened foods add stress and compound fear through guilt, shame, or just plain hypersensitivity.

Choose yourself. Review the demands placed on you and ask how valid they are. Is there the possibility of creating more time for yourself and your needs by eliminating those extra demands on your time and resources? What can be let go? Perhaps you take on way too much due to your inability to say, "No." You want to look good to the boss; you want to please your spouse, kids, and neighbors. Often the cost of this people-pleasing is too high. Your fear is that you will not be okay if you refuse, that you are not safe to do so, and so you sacrifice yourself. If this is so, it's time to make a different choice.

Become ruthless! It is not necessary to be a part of every project and opportunity that comes along. It is possible and wise to decline even good opportunities when they do not support what is most important to you. Say, "No." This is a good time to prioritize. Be your first and only priority. This is not selfish. It creates space so you are available when you are really needed and when it is important to you. When you choose to act, you will have the energy to do so. This is a choice. Many times "no" is a great choice.

In dealing with occasional fear find a health care professional, a trusted friend, or family member with whom to talk. It is ok to ask for reassurance. It is healthy to express your fears and air them out. They can lose their punch when they are verbalized. This does not give license to dwell on it, however. Acknowledge, express, and release!

If fear and insecurity are frequent companions it is time to master them. This process should be quick. Over-thinking will magnify any problem.

- Break the fear down. Make a quick list of every part of the fearful scenario you have built up in your mind.
- Boil down what you fear to its most basic component and face it. What is the fear: failure, success, looking bad, being hurt, *etc.*?
- What is the worst thing that could happen should this fear come to life, that is to say, if what you imagine actually came to pass?
- Face the fear at its simplest level, have courage and make a choice: Faith or fear. Recognize that you are making a choice. Own that choice and its consequences.

Consider the story of Jack (not his real name):

> Jack's dream job has turned into a high-stress, high-demand, little gratitude or appreciation nightmare so common in corporate America. With the job market tight and considering his age, Jack fears he cannot get another job. His boss makes demand after demand and Jack often feels like he is chasing smoke. Part of his job is to imagine every possible bad thing that might happen with the product under development. He is tasked to anticipate and mitigate every possibility. Being

endowed with natural ability from the metal element regarding attention to detail, and the earth element's penchant to worry, he is very thorough. After years of this, Jack's health is suffering. He begins to have panic attacks, he feels like he is dying, and he medicates and isolates himself. His isolation is largely from his family since he cannot seem to change things at work. He will not allow himself to look into other options. He hides in sleep and alcohol, but continues at the grind that work has become. The same boss who victimizes him also rescues him by making sure he is still employed through the company's many layoffs. Gratitude and resentment, fear and anxiety pace his days. Bottom line: Jack is breaking.

What is his major fear? In this case, there are a number of things he fears: job loss, letting down his wife and kids, the possibility of being unemployable due to age, loss of self-respect though much of his self-respect is being sacrificed anyway to his work. The bottom line fear is that he is not good enough. He fears he cannot live up to expectations, especially his own, He fears he will fail. What is the worst thing that could happen? Theoretically, he could lose everything he values.

What are his choices? He could quit the job and leave behind the stressors that consume his essence. Having reclaimed his energy, he could build something else. He is a wonderful writer with a vivid imagination and good sense of humor, he could write a book. He could find a more life supporting employer in his industry or perhaps he could change occupations entirely. With *faith*, energy, and time anything can be created.

What did happen? He stuck it out and his health continued to decline. He had heart trouble which required surgery and finally chronic pain put him on permanent disability. Essentially, he sacrificed his health for his fear. His company tried very hard to cut him off when it became impossible for him to work. There was no support, compassion, and certainly no gratitude for all the years he had allowed the company to bleed him dry.

Now, years later, he is beginning to think about changing his thought processes. Slowly he is turning away from always expecting the worst in every situation. He has started looking toward promise rather than for devastation. He has started using a gratitude list. Every once in a while he remembers how Reiki and prayer stumped the doctors and healed a condition caused by a hospital procedure he went through. He is beginning to remember faith is a better option: faith in the Divine and faith in himself. Perhaps, he is even beginning to see that he is the creator of his own life and that his thoughts are powerful. Slowly he is taking steps to rebuild his life.

Both faith and fear are powerful. Fear paralyzes and weakens. Faith feeds and empowers. You choose.

It is interesting to note that in your pre-life planning, you can anticipate events such as this. You can conspire with the universe to be taken out of a destructive picture if you do not choose to do it for yourself. Disease and disabilities can be just such agreements. It is possible that Jack's disability is the result of one of his pre-life agreements.

Life isn't meant to be lived in fear. Just as Jack is beginning to understand, finding faith can be a matter of remembering. Look back at times in your life when your actions have been powerful, when you felt completely strong and resolved, determined and resourceful. Remember how that felt. Remember how you relied on your inner resources and won. Remember your spiritual connection to that inner resource. Choose to tap into it again. Remember and magnify your resolve and determination to become everything you planned to be in the beginning. Trust that you are supported by life itself.

Feel into the power of water. It flows, it changes, it adapts. Be willing to stay open to change. Flow like the water. Life usually works out even better than you plan if you just let it. The outcome you imagine or desire may involve limits the universe would not include.

Keep learning. Knowledge is a great weapon against fear. Faith is much easier to manage when backed by knowledge. It is easy to fear the snake in a dark room. When the light is turned on, however, you can see the snake you feared is only a rope. Turn on the light. Learn all you can, expand your awareness with greater understanding and trust your own abilities. Find out the facts to inform your choices. Act rather than react.

Give up the need to control. Feeling the need to control and direct everything is a sure sign that you do not feel safe enough to let others play their part. It is really not all up to you. We all play a part. We all need the opportunity to thrive or fail. We all make the choices that create what is. Trying to manage all the choices, to control others, and direct how everything is done denies those around you their right to learn from their choices.

Managing the shadow emotions of the water element could do with a bit of rethinking. Perhaps you could reframe the fear response; you could choose to call it excitement. They are not so dissimilar in the way they actually feel in the body, but feeling excitement allows the mind to be freer to imagine a way into the opportunity that a crisis provides. Excitement can channel energy that may otherwise go into exaggerating the difficulty of a situation and resisting it. Excitement builds possibilities. The connotation is a bit more optimistic and confident. Remember, it is always a choice.

That being said, excitement is still an extreme emotion and can challenge the heart. Develop faith in your ability to survive and even thrive. Compound and grow even small victories, but do so mindfully. It's not about ego, it's about faith. Look at your challenging situations in bite-sized, manageable pieces to make it easier to understand and cope with. Decide on action points which are in line with your capabilities; but realize that you can often expand those capabilities as you move along, especially when you engage your faith.

Do all you can to build your faith in you. Build your energies with rest, good food, play, and exercise. Find your will, that finely tuned part of you that makes it possible to choose *can do* over run away. Connect with something bigger than you be it God, or life force, or your own spirit. Draw strength from that. Use your tools: meditation, affirmations, and breath work (see chapter 8). Above all, recognize that every moment is a choice point.

Questions for Your Journal

- Since emotions affect the physical, there is always some physical sensation that accompanies emotion. When I experience fear, where do I feel it in my body?
- Since everything that happens is an opportunity to choose for my greatest good, what will my new choices be?
- What are examples of my failure to choose becoming a choice?
- What are my new affirmations to remind me that I AM choosing?

Chapter 4

Second Word - Empowerment

"Our deepest fear is not that we are inadequate. Our deepest fear is that we are powerful beyond measure. It is our light, not our darkness that most frightens us. We ask ourselves, "Who am I to be brilliant, gorgeous, talented, fabulous?" Actually, who are you not to be?"
Marianne Williamson,

<u>A Return to Love</u>

Extreme Emotion: Grief

TCM Element: Metal Element

TCM Organ Systems/Meridians: Lungs/Large Intestine

Archetype: Alchemist – Guardian of Change and Transformation

Grief is the second most yin of the extreme emotions. Next to fear, it has the most capacity to turn your world into a whirlpool of inaction and decline. It is so easy to be caught in grief rather than move through it. The feeling of loss can be over-powering. Know that it is important to take the time to honor your experience of grief. Moving through it, however, is essential.

As one might guess in my life of loss in Africa, beside the

shock and anger came huge waves of grief and despair. This is the same feeling that came back to me. It was the surging, pulling, and crushing of the ocean of emotion I was drowning in. I felt shame for not rescuing my people and terrible guilt. Indeed, my heart broke. In this life time I have had a hair trigger response to simple scenes. For example, I remember watching a television commercial of a small child dancing that made me weep. People say I am tender-hearted. The fact is more that I am so intimately connected to what is important from my personal experience that even tiny inconsequential moments gain great importance. My entire approach to being a mother in this lifetime was informed by a deep awareness of what is vital to me because of that loss.

Grief also manifests when you are unable to fulfill yourself. It happens when you sell out your dreams, or when circumstances change and you lose the future that you expected. Most times you only see the ending of what was instead of the new beginning. Rather than allow your emotion to be fluid and do the work of washing away the non-essential, you hold onto the old story and allow disappointment to fester. You fail to see the new path. You become judgmental, dogmatic, or reclusive. You live in the past with your reminiscence, melancholy, and regrets. You focus on details until the bigger picture is gone and personal power is scattered into the depths with the minutia. You get stuck in it. You watch as disappointment and resentment devours your power to adapt, change, and grow. In an attempt to resist and assert control over grief, anything truly important is lost: self-respect, direction, and the ability to move through and forward.

In fact, there is no room for an extended period devoted to woe. In pre-life planning, you sometimes purposely create specific difficult experiences to warn yourself when you are off course. Indeed, sometimes these experiences only happen when you are off course. The important thing to soul is empowering you for your purpose. The constellations of emotions that source from grief are whetting stones for your own empowerment.

It is also true that feelings of entitlement disempower us. Many times feelings of entitlement create the bully and foster resentment and confusion. Consider that we are all equally special. A spark of Creator God is at the source of your being. Since we are all special, none of us is above another. You are not entitled to special consideration, special treatment, or any other special service. A belief in entitlement is a great source of stagnation. It makes you lazy. Feeling entitled would have you wait on rewards you believe you have earned by reason of birth, station, or even through victimization. When your expectations are not met, you grieve over what you thought should have happened.

Staying locked in grief and its offshoot emotions such as loneliness, boredom, feelings of abandonment, reminiscence, self-doubt, neediness, or apathy, keeps you stuck on the wrong side of purpose. These difficult emotions, when they show up in your life, give you important information with which to build something of great value: your own empowered self, based upon what matters to you.

What is power?

If you were lucky as a child, you had parents who taught you with love, reason, and boundaries. This type of parent sets boundaries which allow for creative, active learning with reasonable safety and control. Logical consequences within the parameters of these boundaries are allowed to follow misdeeds so learning happens naturally. Such a parent gives appropriate choices to their child and honors those choices when made. This is a parent who believes in giving *power to* their child. Encouragement and approval, as well as the ability to make choices, empower the child within safe, lovingly enforced boundaries. When treated this way a child tends to feel loved, secure, positive, and successful. This is a "power to" approach.

Unfortunately, many of us were raised with a more "power over" approach. Boundaries may have been arbitrary or flexible, depending on the mood or energy level of the caregiver. They may or may not have been enforced. Consequences were sometimes reflexively harsh, enforced with anger and physical force. Punishment was more common than patience. From the vantage point of a child, what looks like unbridled rage is terrifying. A child's only recourse is to become timid or rebellious. Of course the parent's anger may not have been "rage" but, if the child perceived it that way, the damage is done. Safety becomes a real question in the child's mind. Truthfully, the caregiver may not have known any other way to behave. People follow habitual or learned pathways until they come to realize there is another way.

Most parents mean well and honestly care but do not realize there is such a thing as too much help, too much advice or intervention. This tends to disempower the child. An example of this is the frustrated parent brushing little hands away to tie shoes or dress a child. This makes sense to the adult struggling to get to work. To a child the message is, "I'm not capable." Sometimes a child is intentionally made to feel inadequate or guilty. This is meant to keep the child dependent. Such a caretaker may know no other way to feel personally valuable.

Never intending it, parents create entitlement, mistrust, resentment, lack of confidence, and other compromising attitudes in their children. Rather than trust the child to learn and cooperate parents rush, demand, bribe, punish, criticize, tease, and even belittle. This is quite an unfortunate example to give children. The consequence is that, once the child is grown, these behaviors are taken out to the world at large and reproduced in the form of a bullying boss or judgmental coworker, *etc.* All of the members of your tribe, and the community at large, have had similar experiences. All of us are doing the best we can to cope under the circumstances. Indeed, it seems impossible to escape the influence of the baggage your tribe has brought to bear on you.

This is where empowerment comes in. Empowerment is the essential to taming basic archetypal energies. Due to your conditioning you commonly give your power away or, it is simply taken from you. All your life you are under pressure to submit to higher authority without question. This begs the questions: Do you have any power? How do you use it? Who has power over you? Your archetypal victim energies cause you to believe the power belongs to the big guy, or the boss, the boyfriend/girlfriend, or anybody else. Your child archetype just wants to be taken care of and becomes belligerent or fearful when he or she is the one in charge. You want to feel safe but the prostitute archetypal energies will have you sacrificing your power to get your perceived needs met no matter the cost. Finally the saboteur will tell you, in any voice you will listen to, how powerless and worthless you are. You give your power away and often never realize what you have done. Powerless, you are tossed on the winds of whim and chance. Empowerment is the second word for just this reason: you need to become empowered to combat your myths and become your own higher power.

Metal Element

(Lung and Large Intestine)

"The mysterious powers of fall create dryness in heaven, and they create metal upon earth. Upon the body they create skin and hair, and of the viscera they create the lungs, of the colors they create the white color... and they give to the human voice the ability to weep and to wail. In times of excitement and change, they create a cough. Of the orifices they create the nose with its nostrils; among the flavors they create the pungent flavor; and among the emotions they create grief."

Nei Ching

Lung is the yin organ and large intestine the yang organ of the metal element. The tissue is the skin; the external organ is the nose. When problems with these organ meridians or tissues arise TCM would suggest looking at emotions related to grief which is the extreme emotion associated with these meridians. Related emotions include despair, regret, anxiety, guilt, and shame, *etc.* Coherent emotions, those that direct energies in a more unwavering and stable manner, include integrity, reverence, dignity, respect, acceptance, dependability, inspiration, appreciation, and endurance. The color is white, the sound is crying, and the purging tone is *Shhh* or *Sssss.* Using the color, sound, or purging tones is helpful in releasing and soothing the intensity of grief and its associated emotions.

Health problems associated with the metal element can include breathing problems, coughing, sore throat, voice loss, dry mouth, sinus headache, or shivering. My health problems in this lifetime reflect this intimate relationship with grief. As a baby, for two and a half years I had rheumatic fever, which began with strep throat. When that was over, my childhood was still plagued by sore throats. Later in life I contracted Lyme disease. It proved very difficult to diagnose because my primary symptom was a horrendous cough. Recovery took another two years.

According to TCM, the season for the metal element is late fall: the season of harvest and accounting. This is where an energetic balance sheet of sorts is formed. Certainly, with compromised metal energies my journey in this life has manifested many of the predictable myths: I felt disrespected, not valued by others; I disrespected and undervalued myself. I had many regrets and grudges, judgments and doubts. This combination of physical problems and myths is where my personal energetic balance sheet started. The journey continues.

Many of your coping mechanism *dis*empower you. As one might expect, loss of power creates loss of opportunity without which you cannot have a self-directed and fulfilled life. You cannot grasp a new opportunity if you are buried in misery caused by loss and never look up. Furthermore, coping by acting aloof, putting up walls, or acting indifferent disempowers because the energy needed to create and maintain these façades is so great, failure eventually follows. Personal empowerment is essential for living a self-directed and fulfilling life. Otherwise you are living a shadow life, someone else's life.

Transforming grief leads to empowerment. Grief is the space between no longer and not yet. It is that time between what has ended and whatever comes next. It is important to understand that grief and disappointment are not meant to be full stops in the symphony of life. They are pauses, opportunities to reassess and course correct; and while the ocean of grief threatens to overwhelm, the storm will pass if you let it and you will be richer for knowing what truly matters. That place of understanding, which comes from an awareness of what truly matters, is a foundational place of personal power.

Grief is a great teacher. The waves on an ocean of grief are unavoidable at times. According to Thea Elijah, grief gives you an "aching inventory" of what is really important. It gives an opportunity to find inspiration, dignity, acceptance, and personal power from a heartfelt understanding of what is truly important. Elijah calls this *truing up* to what is unique, treasured, and worthwhile to you in daily life.[4] It also gives you good reason to emphasize and support those things you find to be vital.

Transformation is metal's gift just as empowerment is its goal. If you let it, your grief or disappointment will teach you important things about yourself and your choices. You need to honor your experiences and transform them into life affirming action that is true to your needs and beliefs. Your tribe was able to teach you how they thought you should behave. You have not been taught how to *be* who you are. Claim your power and learn what you meant to be.

---

[4] *METAL: Transform the Virtue of Grief to Righteousness*, Thea Elijah, L.Ac., speech at the Building Bridges Conference

Metal Element Archetype

The Alchemist – Guardian of Change and Transformation

This is where magic happens!

Historically, an alchemist's job was to turn lead into gold. For our purposes, the alchemist's highest goal is complete spiritual transformation. This guardian of change and transformation converts the matter of life into its most sublime and enhanced expression. The alchemist transforms grief into acceptance of what is happening and creates a deep knowing of what is important. Disappointment grows into recognition of other possibilities. You must allow the alchemist in yourself to transform your grief. When this happens, you not only find the ability to endure but also an appreciation of the path, even inspiration from it. You climb to that rarified place where reverence for process, dignity, self-respect, and integrity dwell inside of you. This is your place of power and the home of personal empowerment!

In this place of transformation, the archetypal prostitute has learned to say, "NO!" The saboteur is empowered by that deep awareness of what is most important and warns you of the situations that sidetrack you and consume your power. It helps you to refrain from self-sabotage or from sabotaging others. Your archetypal victim is vigilant to assure you are not exploited and it keeps you out of the victim triangle. The child becomes a playful being that enjoys looking at the world with fresh eyes and finding new inspiration.

Sounds great, right? Even easy! Not so much. How many birthdays have you had? That is how long you have had to establish the habits of thought and practice that now hold you back. Transformation is a journey that requires patience, for you and for your process. Remember the experience of grief and disappointment is meant to transform you and empower your soul journey. Understand the alchemist archetype to appreciate how its energies and impulses inform your life through the metal element.

What Can I Do?

As in all work with and on the extreme emotions, practice *self-care*. (Chapter 8)

In your breathing practice, breathe the color of pure white into your lungs. With each exhale imagine and allow grief, despair, regrets, indifference, boredom, and loneliness to leave with the breath and through the skin. Using *shhh* or *ssss* sounds with the exhale will also help purge the extreme emotions. Always balance purging sounds with breathing in pure white light. Wear white clothing. Let white symbolize the process of purification and "truing up" you are undergoing. When you notice white in your surroundings, use it to remind you of what truly matters in your life. Be grateful for both that awareness and the reminder.

In order to move through the manifestations of grief toward full empowerment, visualize the details of your life as part of a sacred landscape. Your body is its temple. The chambers that are your lungs pull down heavenly air and bring it inside to nourish your life. This air is what you use to communicate through your voice. It energizes all of the body processes by gifting that air to your blood. It is the rarified and intimate connection of what is inside of you to everything else without which there is no life as we know it. Use the connection of breath to look at the sacred landscape of your life.

Breathing is connection unsurpassed. There is much in you to inspire awe, to take you above the mundane world of stumbles and sprains and connect you with the universe. That connection to life, to the Divine, is truly the bigger picture and will help guide you to the infinite possibilities of your own spirit. Connect to your higher-self through breath, prayer, meditation, and stillness to appreciate what is special about you. In these practices you will find inspiration and a path to yourself.

Don't resist your emotions. Breathe deeply into them so they can show themselves to you. Deep breathing keeps grief fluid. It allows grief to move rather than take up residence in the lungs as a cough or the large intestine as constipation or diarrhea. Pay attention to how certain emotions restrict or conflict with lung function and take deep breaths into the belly. Consciously follow the breath as your diaphragm descends and pulls air into the lungs. Breathe in through the nose and out through the mouth. Become aware of how a long breath soothes the rough ocean of emotion. Sigh with the breath. It will take practice to achieve long, smooth breaths if you are currently actively dealing with grief. That's okay, just keep breathing. Long, slow, deep breaths calm stress hormones and decrease tension and anxiety.

Accept that perfection is not the end game. Being a perfectionist flies in the face of understanding what is really there. Nothing is perfect. Nothing can be perfect. Life can be pretty messy. Look around you at how many times you accept the limitations and imperfections of people you love. You know no one is perfect! Still you hold on tenaciously to the myth: I must be perfect, or this must be perfect because I'm in charge of it. Learning to accept what is real, rather than to hold onto some perfect ideal, builds the possibility of self-acceptance, self-appreciation, and, most importantly, empowerment. As it turns out, good enough is often pretty close to perfect!

I am not my story! This simple statement is not a good affirmation, but it is an essential realization. It frees the victim. Realizing you are not defined by the loss of a loved one, a rape, mugging, or child abuse, *etc.* frees you. You are not, after all, only that one experience. Time doesn't begin or end there even if it seems so. There are times of wonder and joy, times of fighting and winning. Writing a whole life story around being victimized is one way to stay stuck in the power of the victim archetype and a reason personal power can be so elusive.

At some point, ruminating over the details of an experience of being victimized must stop. Going over your story again and again re-imprints it and magnifies its energy. In addition, if you are continuing to play the victim for sympathy and/or support, you place all of your power in the past with the perpetrator or tragedy and thereby increase the negative energy around you. At best you get a shallow salve of gratification from the pity of others. Let it go.

"Let it go" is such a common mantra. You see and hear it everywhere. The problem is that just understanding these words intellectually doesn't do much good. Letting go must be an active process. This is especially true since unresolved small disappointments sit quietly and fester. Then, when a big loss occurs, those small disappointments become part of a cumulative whole. This creates a maelstrom of response far out of proportion to what would otherwise have happened. Deal with disappointments large and small as they come up and let them go.

Letting go needs to be active! Every time old habits of grief, despair, defeat, anxiety, *etc.* come up affirm, "I release this, I let it go!" This can be out loud, on paper, or just from the heart. It can be very freeing. One client wrote:

- "I release the dream.
- I release the need to judge the death of that dream.
- I affirm that my soul's purpose is strong and actively growing into fulfillment of my own plan I had for myself before I was born.
- I release the disappointment caused by the death of the dream and recognize everyone's right to experience their journey, their way.
- I am blessed by the death of what was not working and the birth of what is to be.
- I embrace that death is what makes way for birth, a new idea, a new dream.
- I celebrate death for the beginning it is.
- I realize that letting go may cause discomfort in others and myself, but I rejoice in the opportunity to be a catalyst for my journey and for those affected by it.

- I do so only with love.
- I let go. I let God, my soul, my guides illuminate the path."

Another client wrote:

- "I release, I let go of the shame of a child's choice.
- I embrace the small girl so entrapped by obedience she couldn't act on her own behalf.
- I acknowledge this theme in my life and I release, I let go all instances where I was unable to act.
- I send love to all my younger selves who felt like failures.
- I let go, I release the fear of failure. I realize failure is a lesson and a success.
- I acknowledge each step of the lesson. Each failure brings me closer to success.
- I embrace the powerful woman who can now act.
- I acknowledge that I am only rejected when I reject myself.
- I embrace myself completely with love and compassion.
- I forgive my personal fault-finder and judge.
- I embrace them with kindness as the darkness in them melts in the light of my love."

These are positive statements of release written as a flow of consciousness. Each thought prompted the next thought. They can be read again as needed to reinforce the work it took to come to these realizations. They are reminders of a state of being. This attitude can be ingrained permanently with repetition.

Letting go is hardly ever a once and done thing. Be patient with yourself and let things go as often as they comes up. It is often helpful to state, "I let this (situation) go." This is not the same as being in denial. This is a choice to allow the experience to inform you and be gone. Say it out loud or repeat mentally. Whatever it takes to remind yourself that this situation is something you have chosen to release.

Make the hard choice. How many times do you resign your right to choose your own direction? Going along with someone else's plan is often easier. There are fewer risks, less responsibility. Perhaps you feel like you have no choice in a situation and give up, resigning yourself to the situation. Resignation is, in fact, a choice. There is always a choice!

Resignation is passive. Besides disempowerment, resignation eventually creates simmering regret, despair, grief, self-disgust, and defeat. It is true that you must sometimes choose your battles, but if resignation is the response used in most situations, your life will be consumed by some form of grief. If you choose to resign yourself to a situation, you create loss of potential, loss of identity and purpose instead of creating your dream. When you consistently choose to abandon your options and personal desires, things change. Changes can happen so slowly and so thoroughly that your dreams are irretrievably gone before you even know they've been compromised. If you choose to be passive, your dreams are sacrificed to someone else's agenda.

Make life a matter of macro rather than micro sight. Look at the bigger picture. If you are always looking down with your head in the minutia, your imagination becomes atrophied. There is something good to be garnered from every situation. Look at the bigger picture. Imagine how a potentially upsetting circumstance may be a launching pad for something much better, and make that happen. Use your powerful thoughts to create this new dream rather than disappearing into grief and impotence. Look up!

Connect to other people. Do not be solitary. Don't cut yourself off from potential friends and allies. Feeling alone in the world, feeling as if you are the only one suffering, grieving, anxious, or imperfect is all part of the myth. Just as solitude can reflect and imprint inadequacy, self-rejection, and poor self-esteem, companionship can provide feedback and the means to help rise above these cynical and limiting beliefs. Companions will help provide perspective. Find companions with similar interests and goals. Nurture these relationships as you nurture your relationship with yourself. Expect and enjoy imperfections. Wisely chosen companions will applaud when you step into your power.

Respect yourself. Love yourself. Imagine bigger things again. Allow yourself to dream the dream you had for yourself as a child. Check your great critical judge archetype at the door and let yourself be inspired! Your inspiration will provide inspiration for others. Your power to imagine will melt the rigid, moralistic, and judgmental impulses that spin you into the shadow. Your imagination will start the flow toward possibilities. Empower the change! Empowerment creates resilience, leads to self-reliance and knowing you are good enough. When you know you can take care of yourself, it is possible to truly extend that to the world around you.

Empowerment becomes possible when you move through grief, despair, regret, anxiety, guilt, or shame. Empowerment happens as a result of *feeling* these emotions rather than trying to suppress, resist, or control them. Empowerment comes from honoring that the emotions are there, respecting and collecting the lessons they offer, and choosing to move through them. Moving through grief creates strong footing for power based upon what is important to you and that footing is based on your direct experience. Direct experience is not shakable. It creates conviction, ownership of your power, and belief in you. Empowerment means you have the right to choose but, more importantly, that you are *can* choose.

Questions for Your Journal

Empowerment: Alchemy, transformation. Now I can be the alchemist!

- What does empowerment really look like in my life? What would look different in my life if I used my power instead of giving it away?
- Where do I give my power away and to whom?

- Some people are afraid of power. How would owning my power change my perspective? I now know that becoming empowered is a journey I must take to find the full expression of my life. It is how I can embrace the original plan I had for this life, and that plan is always made in love.

- How does having and using power change my personal code of ethics?

- What small disappointments am I holding on to? How can I release them?

- What large disappointments, grief, or resentments am I holding on to? How can I release them?

- How will I choose to empower and recommit to myself?

Chapter 5

Third Word – Commitment

"Every day you must get up, take stock of where you are and ask, "Am I where I want to be? Where do I want to go and how do I get there?" Commitment is having the self-awareness and strength to get up every day willing to course-correct, willing to steer your ship even through the biggest of storms."

Jessica Mitchell, MD, MSc

Extreme Emotion: Worry

TCM Element: Earth Element

TCM Organ Systems/Meridians: Spleen/Stomach

Archetype: Mother, Guardian of Development

How do you feel about yourself right now? Do you welcome attention? Do you believe in yourself or are you riddled with doubt? How much time do you spend thinking about yourself and your problems? Are your needs being met? How much time do you spend thinking about the past? What is your relationship to food? Are you bitter, misunderstood, opinionated? Are you capable of definitive action or are you indecisive? How much time do you spend worrying?

Replace worry with commitment. Cambridge dictionary reports that commitment is, "A willingness to give your time and energy to something that you believe in."[5] In other words, commitment is the basis of a decision to act. If you are empowered, know what is most valuable in life, and are aware of your right to choose, you can replace worry with commitment and create reality from dreams.

Does this sound familiar to you? You have commitments to the external. You are committed to pay for goods and services that support your lifestyle. You have commitments to your friends, family, and your community. Often your commitment to your thought process borders on devotion. Unfortunately, your thought processes do not always serve you; your mind is rarely quiet. You run the same prerecorded tract of thoughts around and around. You mull, you reminisce, you fuss, and you worry, and thus destroy your peace and focus. You don't commit to what is really important.

Worry, at best, dilutes and scatters your energy. At worst, worry magnifies problems. Ruminating over a situation energizes that situation. Your worry feeds it all of your powerful thoughts making it bigger and more complicated. You may be saying you want XYZ to stop but the amount of attention and thought energy you pour into pondering the situation, resisting the outcomes, and agonizing over details makes the universe think that what you want more of *is* XYZ. According to the laws of creation, what you think about and where you direct your energy dictates what you create. What are you creating? What is your commitment?

Often you are committed to your emotional pain. You resist it, you push it away, you deny it, and you never realize just how much this attention feeds the pain. Sometimes you seek help. You reach out to a victim support group. Their purpose is to support a person through a crisis and help them move on. For some people, however,

---

[5] http://dictionary.cambridge.org/dictionary/english/commitment

the support group becomes their new family. Here they find an oasis of understanding and, unfortunately, the new cement to justify and bind them to the pain.

Being committed to your pain and dependent upon those who sympathize with it keeps you from moving through it, beyond it. For some people, the story of their victimization becomes a kind of currency and they take great advantage of it. The ego can be very pleased and gratified by expressions of horror and sympathy. Problem is there is no soul fulfillment that flows from the ego.

What about physical pain? Thoughts, their quality and intensity, do eventually impact your body and it cries out to get your attention. Instead of asking what your pain is trying to tell you, you medicate it away. You suppress it and deny its voice. What story would your pain relate if you listened? What emotion is being stored there? What have you spent so much time ignoring that your body has to shout?

Of course, there are reasons certain physical problems are agreed upon during your pre-birth planning. It is not necessary, however, to manifest all the health possibilities in your plan. That is why humans have free will. A commitment to find and engage actions and thought processes different from your habitual negative ones prevents the need to manifest some of these preplanned health issues.

Commitment is powerful. Do you commit to your emotional wounds or freedom from them? Do you commit to suffering in your physical body or do you use medicine *and* healing practices to heal? Do you commit to complaining and worry or do you commit to action? Applied inappropriately commitment exaggerates life lessons that are less than pleasant. Applied with self-awareness, commitment will move you into line with your soul's plan.

Earth Element

(Spleen and Stomach)

"The mysterious powers of the earth create humidity in heaven and fertile soil upon earth. They create the flesh within the body, and of the viscera they create the stomach [and spleen]. Of the colors they create the yellow color... and they give to the human voice the ability to sing. In times of excitement and change they cause the emission of belching. Of the orifices they create the mouth; of the flavors they create the sweet flavor: and of the emotions they create consideration and sympathy."

Nei Ching

The earth element organs are the spleen (yin) and the stomach (yang). The tissue is said to be flesh/muscle, and the sense organ is the tongue. According to TCM, issues in these areas could be ameliorated by attending to the extreme emotions associated with the earth element namely: worry, regret, reminiscence, self-doubt, self-absorption, and neediness. Coherent emotions and abilities (those which cause less confusion) include trust, openness, empathy, deep knowing of security and stability, nourishment, altruism, and service. Potential health problems from imbalance of this element include weight problems, digestive upsets, headaches, and poor sleep. The color is yellow, the sound is singing, and the purging tone is "Ho." Using color, sound, and purging tones is helpful in releasing and soothing the intensity of earth element extreme emotions.

Earth element energies are reflected by the great mother that is our planet. Her bounty and beauty supplies us magnificently. How is it then, that we worry there isn't enough? We buy into the myth of lack with such commitment that we perceive life as lacking. We create lack. We become selfish and apprehensive. We complain and worry and chew on our opinions as if they define absolute truth. We become martyrs in our minds and, while we seek attention and understanding, we reject any attention and understanding we might get as inadequate or insincere. Instead of bounty we create bitterness, misery, and regret.

For many of us, worry is our morning coffee. We reminisce about how things used to be, rejecting how things are. We worry about time, money, jobs, how we look, and even what someone else might think about how we look. We become apprehensive and have a nagging ball of something (worry? fear?) in the pit of our stomach that only feels better when we feed it, or when we don't feed it. Weight issues, too fat or too skinny, abound though the supposed fat or skinny person often has no idea of how they really look. Weight issues, insecurity, self-doubt, and neediness all happens because we are out of touch. We are out of touch with ourselves and out of touch with earth energies.

We are suffering from too much pressure of experience or, perhaps, exposure. Our personal myths are supercharged due, in part, to the input of the news media and corporate engineering of our self-image based on profits. We buy into the movie and modeling industries' portrayal of what makes the perfect person. Our role models have become impossibly tough guys from someone's imagination or beauty queens. Their blemishes are airbrushed away, their legs are lengthened and bulges are added or subtracted, depending on the situation. Sadly, we don't even seem to understand that we have been sold lies. We are pummeled with news stories and movies about people doing horrible things. News is fed to us with the proper 'spin' so can we watch big business and political leaders exploiting us and we do not even blink about it. Our sense of right and wrong is challenged so often in the name of news and entertainment that we have become desensitized to violence. Our values are in question. In the meantime, our children are getting a skewed version of what it takes to be "okay" on this planet; and worry becomes our bread and butter.

Basically, we have forgotten how to accept things as they are and move forward. We believe in doom and gloom. We believe that it's a struggle to exist, that there isn't enough money, or attention, or (pick something) until we can no longer see ourselves as the divine creations that we are. We no longer understand the close connection we have with each other as travelers on this planet. We buy into myths and they send us into the tailspin of worry, anxiety and suspicion. We no longer know what to believe or how to act. We are involved in living on the surface of life without a commitment to its depths. Worry causes us to go through the motions of living while frittering away opportunities.

Commitment is the key to moving forward out of worry and indecision. Action without commitment is weak and poorly aimed. Making commitments allows you to arm against unevolved earth element energies that scatter your ability to make progress toward your goals! Commitment is also critical to having a life of your own making. Rather than accepting Shakespeare's proverbial "slings and arrows of outrageous fortune," you create your fortune, outrageous or otherwise, with your thoughts and actions. Therefore, a commitment to act with integrity according to your beliefs is what it takes to define and shape your world the way you want it to be.

"Apprehension and anxiety, worries and preoccupation – normal movement of thoughts and reflection becomes a disturbance that deepens and attacks the Spirits..."

Huangdi Neijing

Worry creates much of the drama in life and many of us are in love with that drama. Even though drama makes you miserable, you hesitate to move beyond it because it is what you know. Reliving or rehashing old wounds and slights is usually habitual and definitely far from productive. This is worry, also known as thought power on overdrive. Constant worry directs all your energy into the past where it will do no good. It projects the past onto the future weaving fear and apprehension into your life story. Worry keeps you stuck. You need to live now, in present time, without the drama.

The shamans of Peru honor the serpent energy of the south. Their guidance is to shed the past the way the serpent sheds her skin. This is good advice. Shedding the past doesn't take away the lessons or the memory. Instead it takes away the weight of the baggage you carry around as a result of the memory. This diminishes the impact of the past on the present and on the future.

Jill (not her real name), a sweet woman at a course I attended, demonstrated earth energies perfectly. She orchestrated a workshop that seemed to have several moving parts over most of two weeks. She arranged for venue, housing, transportation, food, t-shirts, and vendors. She hired musicians and planned a party to honor the presenter complete with special foods. She worked endlessly. She always asked what she could do to help you, make your stay better, or solve any problem that may have come up. The presenter, on the other hand, was a prickly kind of person, judgmental and dissatisfied. Even the wonderful party held in her honor was somehow lacking and this sent Jill into a dither. In the middle of all this Jill suffered a death in her close family. She was beset by worry and indecision. Her commitment to the course prevented her from honoring her commitment to her family. She wondered how she could possibly leave to attend to her family. Finally we had to almost force her out the door.

Earth energies, as you might guess from this story, are about nurture. A person with strong earth energies that are out of balance will want to fuss and scheme to make everything right. Anxiety and self-doubt plague them. They feel they cannot do enough for others and that whatever they do is not good enough. They feel everything is up to them; no one else can do it correctly or they don't want to impose. They want to fix everything for everybody. Jill was grieving, tired, frustrated, and she rejected help. She also carried some extra weight as is common for people who try to console themselves with food.

Earth Element Archetype

Mother: Guardian of Development

Understanding the scope of the earth element archetype will help define the energy and impulses this element brings into your life. What could be more appropriate than mother as an archetype for the earth element? In her light aspects she is the life giver and nurturer. She shows patience, caring, and unconditional love. An empowered mother teaches by allowing learning to happen within lovingly enforced boundaries. On the shadow side she is needy, uncertain; she is a martyr. She is overbearing and controlling, devouring, and abusive. As with all archetypes, the side you recognize is very revealing about where your personal attitudes need to be examined.

How you commit to yourself and your plan for this life makes all the difference. An effective mother uses her ability to plan and nurtures every aspect of life. She puts aside worry in a commitment to the greater good of herself and, thereby, those under her care. She realizes that her first priority must be to herself, otherwise, there will be nothing to give to others. She knows that taking care of herself is not the same as being indulgent with herself. Use the mother archetype to help you surrender to a commitment to be the most loving, nurturing, and altruistic person possible. The gift of that commitment naturally extends to all of us walking with you on this journey of life. Your example of self-love will teach others how to love and nurture.

What Can I Do?

Jill tried to take care of everyone but herself. Always practice *self-care* first (chapter 8). When you are feeling better, your world seems brighter and you have more to give.

Yellow is a bright, happy color. In the world of color therapy yellow stimulates mental ability, concentration, confidence, and aids positive feelings. It is hard to worry when you are wrapped in yellow and being creative. Dress happily and sing through your worries. In your breathing practices, breathe the color yellow into your spleen on the left side of your body. With each exhale imagine and allow worry, regrets, self-doubt, and anxiousness to leave with the breath. Using the "Ho" sound with the exhale will also help purge extreme emotions. Always balance the purging sounds with breathing in pure yellow light.

Cultivate optimistic realism. Optimism flies in the face of worry. You cannot be optimistic and worry at the same time. Be realistic about what is possible but always expect the best. A true optimist isn't about the proverbial pie in the sky, but he or she does expect things to work out for the best. He or She also realizes that *the best* isn't necessarily easy nor does it always look as expected. That is realism.

Tell the universe that you want more of the good things in your life by acknowledging what you have to be grateful for. Practice gratitude. Be thankful for everything big or small. Mother Earth is generous. Acknowledge her gifts to you by practicing gratitude. Every life has something beautiful about it. There is always something to be grateful for. The best part of gratitude is, once you start expressing it, you find more and more things to be grateful for. Count each one. Make a list and add something new to it every day. Recite this gratitude list often to remind you of all the good in your life.

When you find things to be grateful for, you realize there is less time and reason for obsessiveness and worry. Recite your gratitude list as soon as your habitual worry tract starts playing in your mind. This short circuits the negative thoughts. Recite your gratitude list to help you wake up or fall asleep. Expand your gratitude list while you wait in traffic. Everything that happens does so for a reason; slow traffic may just be keeping you out of a dangerous situation. Recognize this gift and be grateful. Any excuse taken to appreciate the bounty and beauty of life will reward you with feelings of trust, acceptance, and caring.

Stop worrying! Gratitude can short circuit the tailspin of worry but it doesn't change that there are things you need to take care of. You need to address these things when there is a problem. When you are worried, do the following:

- Set a time limit on how much time you spend evaluating your situation.
- Put it on paper. List each component of your concern. You can't list the same thing more than once. If you come to a stop and can't readily think of another thing, you are done. Do not dither and fuss over the points on the list; you have a time limit.
- What are you trying to achieve by addressing this problem? What is the goal?
- Ask yourself how important the overall goal is to the growth of your spirit. This constitutes a reality check.
- Next, assign weight to each item. Decide quickly. This is highly personal, but is not to be agonized over. Put down your first response. Your gut reaction is most often the correct one.
- Now that you have your list and know what parts of it are important, you can decide what you actually have control over. Be realistic. You do not control everything.
- If something is within your power, act. Make a plan. What are the steps you must take to reach the goal? Again, itemize the steps. Be prepared to make necessary adjustments as you move through your plan.
- If an item is not within your control, choose to work around it like water does or let it go.
- ACT! *Commit to the goal and follow through with the plan.*
- Reevaluate as necessary, and course correct if needed. Realize whatever happens is a gift. If it goes the way you imagine, you win. If it goes another way, it can be better than you could have imagined so you win. If not, you learn, so you also win!

This is the essence of commitment: Have a plan and follow it through. Put energy into your plan and soon that energy will build. Putting energy into the plan and moving forward multiplies positive energy, just as putting energy into worry increases worry! Choose where you want your energy to go. Commit!

Ground yourself. You have probably seen people who are flighty and stuck in what seems to be another world. They cannot settle their energies, have scattered thinking, and ineffective actions. These people are not grounded. Our culture seems to admire people who have their "feet on the ground." Being grounded means that you are in touch with what is real, not stuck in the past or worried about the future. It means that your place of power and creativity is here right now and you are in touch with that power. Being grounded means you have found the foundation for commitment and the fulfillment of your dreams. It means you will be able to implement steps toward those dreams.

Bringing your dreams into reality only happens when you can ground the energy of that dream. It's like planting a tree. It must have roots to flourish. It must be planted. Your commitment to your dreams needs to be grounded. Following is a simple exercises to help you ground. Find a quiet place when you first try this.

> Make yourself comfortable either sitting or standing. Close your eyes and allow your energy to settle. Next, imagine roots sprouting out of your feet and growing into the deepest parts of the earth. As the roots grow longer and longer, begin to feel and imagine the warmth at the core of the planet. Feel the earth's vital energies enter your roots and come into you. Breathe these energies up into your body. Feel the strength of these energies in your body. Allow the energy to fill your body with warmth. Allow the warmth to relieve and release the emotions that are holding you back. Imagine

and feel worries and scattered thinking flow out of your roots to be purified in the heat that nourishes you. Feel strength settle into your being.

Breathe.

Truly feel your connection to the ground and imagine how it is to walk connected to the earth's essence. When you are ready, open your eyes and walk. Continue to be aware of your roots as you walk. Your roots move effortlessly through the rich, dark, earth with you as you move. Hold on to the awareness of this connection and reestablish it whenever you begin to feel scattered.

With practice you will be able to ground anywhere. Reconnect with your awareness of this relationship to the physical earth as you go through your day. Being grounded helps you stay present and it helps you remember what is real. From this foundation, dreams can be made into reality.

For someone who is full of regret, or who spends much of their available time reminiscing, there is no energy or inclination for commitment. People filled with self-doubt, who are self-absorbed, or needy have out of balance earth element energies. These people see lack, perhaps out of habit. They may believe they have nothing to contribute or that they are not worthy enough to make a contribution. They lack true commitment to themselves and others. There is an aching hole which cannot be filled, and while they may be involved in life, struggling to please, they are not committed to the full expression of it. Indeed, they do not understand how. They are not grounded in the present and its possibilities. They fail to nurture themselves. This is the biggest mistake anyone can make. A commitment to yourself and developing your divine potential is the most important one you have.

Eating disorders are often found in people with out of balance earth element energies. This is eating (or not eating) as therapy or punishment. It is a tough way to treat yourself. Earth energies are about nurture. Harsh self-judgments and guilt make some people punish themselves by not eating while others, seeking comfort or protection, eat everything in sight, whether hungry or not. Worry, anxiety, and self-loathing result in binging/purging, anorexia, or uncontrolled appetite. Don't be afraid to seek professional help. Additionally, you can try the following tips:

- Use eating as an opportunity to meditate by eating mindfully. Savor each bite, eat slowly, chew thoroughly, and be calm and relaxed about it. When your mind wanders, bring it back to the practice of eating mindfully.

- Minimize distraction; for example, don't watch television while you eat. This takes eating out of the realm of robotic consumption and allows you to recognize you *are* eating and that you can enjoy it. It will also help you realize when you are full.

- Watch what you eat, but if you have decided to eat something you consider forbidden, intentionally *commit* to its complete enjoyment! Eat it slowly and savor every mouthful. Eating is required; it is not a reward or a punishment. Do not allow yourself to use it as such.

- Make healthy, whole food choices. Eliminate sweets and over-processed packaged foods from your diet. These foods are addictive and aggravate anxious feelings. Marty (not her real name) made snickerdoodle cookies for her children almost daily but ate most of them herself. Invariably, the next day she felt nervous and jumpy until she made more snickerdoodles and ate them. Sugar and other carbohydrates found in junk food are addictive. They change mood and blood chemistry. Again, be sure to commit to healthy, whole food choices.

- Avoid artificial sweeteners. They are not your friends.

- Antacids can contribute to malabsorption and nutritional deficiencies. Interestingly enough, Marty eventually realized that the sweets she ate contributed to headaches and her need for antacids.

- When you need antibiotics, take them but be aware they also compromise digestive health by killing good bacteria along with the bad. Taking probiotics and enzymes helps correct such problems. Again, be aware of what you put in your body.
- Substitute inappropriate eating with activities. Play! Dig into art, horseback riding, tennis, skiing, chess, yoga, or whatever it is that helps you feel better about your place in the world. Make a date with yourself. Put it on the calendar. Commit to doing something enjoyable often, if not daily.

Give yourself some credit. There were times in your life when you felt capable and confident. Find that. Feel that. Take a moment to feed that feeling of capability and confidence with your thoughts. Re-experience that. You are capable and confident! Don't listen to your personal myth that says otherwise. Make a list of things that make you feel good about you. What is beautiful about you, whether recognized by others or not? What is special about you? Acknowledge these things, put them in writing, and own them. It doesn't matter what others think about you. That is their business, not yours.

Connect with empathy. According to Psychology Today, "Empathy is the experience of understanding another person's condition from their perspective; you place yourself in their shoes and feel what they are feeling."[6] Feeling empathy isn't about feeling sorry for someone. Empathy is about understanding and appreciating the experience of a brother or sister in the family of man. This is a more cosmic vision than a personal one; it takes in a bigger picture. It lends perspective and allows you to resonate with that part of yourself you see in the other person. Empathy begins when you appreciate your own inner worth as well as your

---

[6] www.psychologytoday.com/basis/empathy

challenges. Then you can recognize the worth of every living being on the planet.

Find ways to be of service. Recognize that your needs are always met. If you doubt it, check your gratitude list. Once you have that awareness you can be honestly caring, understanding, and responsive to the needs of others. Make a commitment to volunteer. Go in person to a soup kitchen or homeless shelter and put in some time helping. This will enrich you much more than just sending a check to charity or throwing a dollar in the Salvation Army pot at Christmas. Giving of yourself allows your heart to expand. It adds to your gratitude list. It helps you to see where life is good and, sometimes, where life really is hard. Again, it develops perspective. Develop a true desire to help others and you will be surprised at how much comes back to you. Help offered from the heart is not a duty; it is a gift that goes both ways.

The coherent (constructive) energies from the earth element are commitment, open-heartedness, trust, acceptance, empathy, altruism, and service. Commit! You get into trouble because you fail to act. Doing something, even if it is wrong, creates movement. You can learn from your mistakes. Make a commitment to yourself and your personal well-being. Your commitment to self serves all of mankind. We are all connected. We are the sum of each personal part. Commit to action; it is essential to building a life free of worry. Control what you can and let the rest go. Be as positive about your life as you can. Accept your truth instead of believing what others tell you. Amplify coherent earth element energies with gratitude. Commit to living your best life.

Questions for Your Journal

- What am I worried about? What concerns keep me sleepless or unproductive?
- How can I apply the nurturer to myself regarding my concerns? How can I *commit* to the processes and tasks that I choose?
- How much time do I spend day dreaming or thinking back over my life? What can I do to bring my energy into the present?
- What is my commitment to myself? What activities, projects, or dreams make me feel eager to get up in the morning? Which feed my spirit like no other? How can I commit to them, and thus, to myself?
- My commitment to myself makes my blessings grow. I was misinformed when I thought there wasn't enough, when I was needy, when I longed for nourishment for my spirit. For what am I grateful? What feeds me now? My gratitude list is unending; this is my list: (Begin making your list.)

Chapter 6

Fourth Word – Boundaries

"No" is a complete sentence.

Unknown

Extreme Emotion: Shock

TCM Element: Fire Element

TCM Organ Systems/Meridians: Heart/Small Intestine,
Pericardium/Triple Burner

Archetypes: Lover, Guardian of Creation
Protector, Guardian of Integrity

Naturally, when talking about the heart the first question is, "What about love?" Love is *not* an extreme emotion. Love is the initial emotion. Love is the essence of all creation. In other words, all of creation is an expression of love. The Tao describes that impulse, "Tao gives birth to one, one gives birth to two, two gives birth to three, three gives birth to ten thousand beings."[7] Everything in creation came from one essential expression of love. All of

---

[7] http://www.taomanor.org/10000.html

creation is love, as are all emotions. No matter how distorted and unrecognizable love may have become, all of creation is essentially made up of it. All feelings are descended from love; yes, even the ugly ones. To rediscover love, contain it, purify it, and to distill it back to its essence you need boundaries.

The heart and pericardium are so closely tied together that TCM includes both under the fire element. Many sources name joy as the extreme emotion of the heart. Joy is not necessarily frenzied or out of control, however, so the extreme emotion for our purposes is shock caused by excessive excitement. Any shock, even excessive joy, can challenge the heart. This excitement can be from good or bad experiences. In a similar way, the pericardium, as the protective mechanism of the actual heart, is susceptible to shock. Sudden extreme joy or tragedy can impact the pericardium and disturb the heart. Jumbling the heart energies with extremes creates restlessness, self-doubt, elation, despair, or anxiety (though anxiety is also a symptom of earth element imbalances.)

Stress (aka shock) has been named the culprit in heart trouble for some time. After all, life can be fast and furious. How is it possible to sort through it all? How can one possibly survive the maelstrom of information, demands, imperatives, and catastrophes that occur on a daily basis? More importantly one might ask, "How do I ever find me and fulfill my needs through the chaos that is my environment? How do I deal with the horrific impact of everyday stress here, in my heart, where I live?" The answer is boundaries.

You may ask how boundaries could ever allow you to rediscover, contain, purify, and distill essential love. Boundaries do the trick because they cut out the extra noise around and inside you. Boundaries allow you to find and work on what is truly important. They give you time to look into the voices of myths and limitations you have thus far just accepted. With time, you can discover what is actually true about yourself. At that point, you have enough pertinent information to develop your own approach to behavior, goals, and acceptability. Boundaries make room for you by keeping other people's agendas from taking over your life. They give you time to think and to sort through your concerns and inner dialogue. With time to think you can discover your own dreams. You can decide how to make a commitment to those dreams and to yourself. You can figure out what your soul wants from you and get back to love.

Boundaries inform and define an individual. Healthy boundaries are set by people who know themselves and who have the courage to own their destiny. Such people choose what behavior is acceptable both to and from others. People with healthy boundaries realize that blame, guilt, and shame are often programmed by the tribe or imposed rather than earned. They also realize that, while responsibility for their lives and actions is theirs alone, they are not accountable for anyone else's actions. They determine what consequence someone else's actions have on them and how they will respond.

Basically, each human being is responsible to and for themselves. Sometimes this knowledge is hard to hold on to under the pressure of peers as Kris (not her real name) found out. Kris is a bright kid, good in school, eager to please, and lonely. Saying, "no" to a group of popular kids who wanted her to do their homework for them was, at best, difficult. One part of her (the saboteur) said, "Come on, Stupid, agree! This is your chance to show them what you're worth. If you don't, you'll be alone forever." Believing the voice of the saboteur spouting her personal myths, Kris agreed to help them. At this point Kris has allowed the prostitute to dictate; she is selling her mental ability for the hope of gaining acceptance into the popular group. Kris hoped for friendship and approbation. What she got instead was closer to ridicule. She was given more and more to do for them and was too busy doing it to be included in their activities. Slowly Kris realized that she was being used. There was no connection; these *friends* mocked her behind her back. She felt betrayed. She had become a victim.

"No" is a simple word, yet it is the magic word for setting

boundaries. The story above illustrates how archetypal energies work. Archetypal energies such as described for Kris, create situations that allow you to find your will (or will not). Fortunately, there are many such opportunities presented to you in business, school, among peers, or partnerships. It is fortunate because these experiences allow you to flex your "NO" muscle.

To get an experience and awareness of boundaries, workshop participants took turns standing at one end of the room facing away from the rest of the class. It was the beginning of the course so the students did not know their classmates. Class members were asked to approach the student facing away one at a time. The person being approached did not know who was coming toward them. They were just told to raise a hand when they noticed or became concerned about the changing energies caused by the approach of the classmate. Results showed a wide range of responses. One woman allowed anyone to approach until they were right on top of her. Some consistently allowed women to get closer than men and vice versa. Some stopped classmates almost immediately. Reaction to this experiment surprised the participants. One self-assured lady was shocked at the distance to which she held men. Another had no idea that allowing everyone close was not good for her. This is a simple thing to try with a group of acquaintances. It will lend insight into your personal space and the boundaries you set around it.

Protective walls you build around your heart after you have been hurt are boundaries of a sort. This type of boundary is reactionary and exclusionary. It will preclude any possibility of honest future relationships. If a relationship does form, reactionary boundaries can even predetermine the outcome of the relationship. This is the type of boundary I constructed at one point in this life. The Simon and Garfunkle song, *I Am a Rock*, became my theme song. I don't believe there was a great hurt in this life, but I felt a general rejection from people around me. I felt rejected and judged by my church. My father was certainly looked down upon and other members of my family had life experiences that garnered harsh judgments from fellow church members. I didn't want to be rejected and hurt anymore but I also didn't believe I was worthy of any good coming to me. I rejected myself. Old stories die hard. At that point, I didn't really even know that I had old stories, just that I was not comfortable or particularly wanted. My protective boundaries created effective isolation.

It is difficult to grasp the notion that we are temples, not tarmac. Your physical, mental, emotional, and spiritual assets are not up for grabs on the open market unless you allow it. It is your responsibility to examine all of the information you have been given throughout your life. You must choose what part of it really applies to your soul; what part is true to your own inner heart. You need to decide what boundaries will support, rather than exploit, your temple. Having healthy boundaries does not guarantee you will never be hurt. They do, however, reduce your chances of becoming a victim or of missing out on life hiding behind your protective walls.

Real boundaries are not reactionary. They are in place to protect you from your own excesses and from the need to react to the outside world. You must place good boundaries on your inner life. For example, place a boundary that limits your inner dialog so that worry doesn't spin you into inaction.

Good boundaries are definitely limits imposed on external demands. These are created through conscious consideration about what is acceptable to you. You place boundaries on your interactions with others based on your goals, beliefs, and expectations. These are premade choice points, not cast in stone, but guidelines to insure that your personal integrity is uncompromised. Good boundaries help you stay on course and not be diverted into situations that compromise you, take advantage of you, or even just use your energies in a manner that doesn't support you. Jill, the event planner described in the previous chapter, would have acted much differently had she had good boundaries. Instead of trying to say yes to every demand and worrying about staying at the party, Jill would have said firmly that she needed to leave, and she would have gone. Good boundaries help keep your energies focused on things that are truly important and allow you to change direction if needed.

The best part is: you get to decide what is truly important to you. An adult who seeks permission from the boss, the spouse, or anyone else is giving their power away. They are still acting from the child's perspective. Growing up means you get to question! You get to decide for yourself and enjoy the consequences. When you have good boundaries, you realize that often it is necessary to say, "No." You give yourself permission to be an adult and to say, "No" without justifying the decision; your reasons can be your own. "No" is the magic word of boundary setting!

Fire Element

Heart / Small Intestine
And
Pericardium / Triple Burner

"The mysterious powers of summer create heat in the heaven and fire upon earth. They create the pulse within the body and the heart within the viscera. Of the colors they create the red color…and they give to the human voice the ability to express joy. In times of excitement and change they grant the capacity for sadness. Of the orifices they create the mouth with it the palate: of the flavors they create the bitter flavor: of the emotions they create happiness and joy."

Nei Ching

Organs associated with the fire element in Chinese medicine are the heart and pericardium (yin) and the small Intestine and triple burner (yang). Tissues associated with the heart are the vessels; its sense organ is the tongue. This information is useful when you are uncertain which emotion is causing an imbalance. Check the problem areas, organs and tissues for clues. As mentioned earlier some of the extreme emotions for the heart include restlessness, self-doubt, elation, despair or anxiety. Coherent emotions include joy, self-confidence, self-respect, and happiness. The sound is laughing, the color red, and tone "Haa". Using the sound, color, and tone in your healing practice helps to release and soothe excessive fire energies. Fire is the most yang of all the elements though there is still some yin. Fire corresponds with summer.

The heart is the center of the body/mind and as such may be thought of as the emperor. The emperor's job is to oversee the smooth and harmonious workings in the landscape of the human body. The emperor is aided by the treasurer or minister of reception (small intestine) who takes care of the minutia and attends to detail. This minister refines and separates the pure from the impure, assimilating what is needed, and passing the rest on for elimination. This job requires clarity of thought and powers of discernment.

Traditionally there are two other associations with the heart: the pericardium and the triple burner. Protecting the emperor falls to the "king's bodyguard" or pericardium. In fact, the pericardium does protect the heart physically. Chinese medicine also assigns it the duty of protecting the heart from excess of emotion. The triple burner is not an organ *per se* but a functional energy system involved in regulating the activities of other organs. The upper burner (thorax cavity, mouth to stomach) controls intake, the middle burner (abdomen, stomach to pyloric valve) controls transformation, and the lower burner (pelvis, pyloric valve to anus) controls elimination. The Triple Burner is said to regulate consciousness and when consciousness is stable, intent is benevolent and kindhearted.

The extreme emotions associated with the heart include shock, vulnerability, nervousness, anxiety, mania, excitability, coldness, aloofness, or indifference. Physical manifestations of imbalance of these energies range from hyperactivity to inertia. You can experience irregular heartbeats and chest pain. You could become hypertensive, experience dizziness, or get irritable bowel, cramps, diarrhea, or constipation. By contrast, the coherent emotions are open-heartedness, peace, contentment, joy, intimacy, tranquility, expressiveness, expansiveness, optimism, and hope.

Clearly, in my life in Africa, my first response was shock. I could still feel it on that day of the class; I became intimately acquainted with madness. Many people suffer shock in this world: soldiers, accident or crime victims. How does one cope with the unthinkable? For these people, with trauma so close at hand, professional help is required. Eventually, however, some semblance of sanity returns and you can begin the long journey back to balance.

It is naïve to think that personal boundaries would have helped me or anyone else in that moment when we were ultimately violated. Perhaps this is the gift: after trauma, it is possible to clarify just where your boundaries need to be. In that one moment of destruction, anything that is not valuable, not essential in your life is stripped away from your awareness; only that which is of ultimate value remains. When you know what is of ultimate value, you know your ground. You know what needs to be protected. You can find and set your boundaries.

Even without great trauma it is essential to set boundaries. You need to define and defend what is acceptable and unacceptable to you based on your own values. Effective boundaries allow you to focus on the important aspects of your life and diminish the drain on your resources caused by thinking anyone else is more important. You become less vulnerable or, perhaps more importantly, you choose where to be vulnerable. It is much easier to say "no" when you have firmly in your mind exactly what is worth your attention.

Fire Element Archetypes

LOVER: Guardian of Creation
and
PROTECTOR: Guardian of Integrity

The fire element cultivates appreciation for forces that

influence the organization of your life and environment. In the hope of managing unnecessary stressors, excessive excitement, and shock, boundaries direct that fiery energy so it can be used to raise appreciation of your true self and direction. It is important to understand how the following archetypes help define the energies and impulses of the fire element.

A lover archetype is generally thought of as those who are romantically inclined and/or who exhibit great devotion for art, music, or nature, *etc.* and, as such, is a guardian of passion. Where it regards the fire element the archetypal lover is the Guardian of Creation. In addition to passion, the lover creates and oversees the development of self-love and self-respect as these are needed to produce balanced and effective fire element energies and healthy boundaries.

When the lover archetype is not well developed, its shadow fertilizes the ground for problems with the survival archetypes because so much of its energy involves self-esteem, or its lack:

- Consider the child archetype. It includes great energy for expansion and creativity but children are defenseless. They are easily crushed by adults too busy, unaware, or unconcerned to care. As a consequence, when they grow up, they feel confused, abandoned, and unworthy. A whole cascade of emotions, impressions and responses come out of the experience. Too often, these children grow into the same habits as the adults who helped squander their potential.

- The saboteur archetype attacks the heart through challenges to self-esteem. Saboteur energy tries to feed you all the reasons you are not good enough, strong enough, pretty enough, smart enough, *etc.* and you believe it. Finally you don the masks of indifference or aloofness. You worry and/or resign yourself to your fate. You medicate or drink away the anger or depression caused by these myths of your insufficiency.

- For love, acceptance, or security, the prostitute archetype ends up in untenable situations. He does work he cannot stand to do because he needs the money. She settles for crumbs in a relationship instead of leaving. The prostitute justifies and excuses, but never limits how others can use them. No boundaries are set. Everything is impacted: body, mind, emotions, and spirit.

- While a victim can most certainly be made by circumstance, it is possible to get a little too comfortable with it. Indeed, some people settle into victimhood and set up camp. It takes great courage to move through victimization. Some victims do not want to move out of support group settings and continue on with their life. These people feel like they finally belong and are cared for. They are gratified by the sympathy they receive.

The protector archetype is similar to the knight archetype. Both of these archetypes have spiritual overtones of service and devotion and can be called the guardians of integrity. While the knight's virtues are loyalty and self-sacrifice, the protector's virtue for our purposes must be loyalty to and love of the self. This is not about ego! When finely tuned, the protector allies with the soul's growth plan to help maintain boundaries necessary to create space to grow into the full expression of your soul. The ability to honor the soul's intention for life will stabilize and protect you from stressors that would eat away at your ability to grow and prosper. The mechanism to pursue and protect your soul's plan without compromise is boundaries.

Your heart is the home of the fire element; boundaries are the container. When heart fire is supported and sustained properly, it will burn away confusion and myths. Through your will and strength of spirit you are able to become open-hearted. You gain perspective and find understanding to inspire your efforts to live with your heart open. By lovingly discovering the truth about what is appropriate and true for you, you silence the saboteur.

You give yourself permission to own the truth of your larger self. The prostitute and victim both say, "No more!" As an adult you reach your inner child and feed it the love and acceptance you may have heretofore done without. Find the courage to set and respect boundaries, your own and those of others.

What Can I Do?

Surround yourself with beauty in whatever form you enjoy and practice self-care as is written about in Chapter 8. Especially after trauma, an accident, an ugly divorce, a stressful day, or whatever it is, your priority must be you!

Use a red color choice in your clothing if you are feeling low and a quieter pale pink if you are overwhelmed. Both will support the heart. Breathe the color into your heart any time you need a soothing boost; then breathe out the distressing emotions that are causing problems. Turn the radio up in the car and sing a great song! Express your feelings through your song. Let your feelings out.

Take stock. Do you believe that you are loveable and worthy, or are you like Jill and the woman in the workshop who didn't make themselves a priority? Whether you know it or not, the answer is, yes, you are loveable and worthy. This is a point you must come to own. Trust the affections of those who love you. Trust your own ability to love, to be discerning rather than judgmental. Trust and discernment can be developed and are conscious choices you must make. Cultivate these feelings intentionally with affirmations and personal prayers or rituals as suits your personality and beliefs. Allow yourself to believe the possibility that judgements of your failure, your worthlessness, and your unlovable-ness are myths. Give yourself permission to find out what is valuable and worth your time.

Create boundaries that affirm your worth and prevent the distractions which otherwise would consume you. Be picky. Don't allow others to tempt you with their pet projects. It is not necessary to undertake every task just because someone asked you. In fact, you may find yourself saying no to good opportunities just so that you have time for great ones!

Develop perspective. Realize that not all bad outcomes are negative. Sometimes failure makes room for something better that wouldn't or couldn't happen without the death of the failed situation. For example, a new fulfilling relationship can come into your life once the energy spent chasing an old or destructive relationship is reclaimed. Cut your losses on the bad relationship and learn the lessons that relationship offered. When you understand and own those lessons, you can build a new relationship on better footing. Learn from the past, raise your awareness, and set your boundaries so you do not have to repeat the lesson.

Life depends on your point of view, on perspective. There is a good children's story about perspective. Several mice describe a great thing that has taken up space in their home. To each it looks different. The mice living above the new thing describe it one way while the mice living behind describe something much different. The description varies depending on the position of the mice, above, behind, to the front, or to the side. Each has its own experience with the new thing. Finally it is revealed that they are all seeing the same cow. Perspective tells the mouse living above the cow that the air is warm and cozy with it there, while the one at the back speaks of danger.

Learn to look at all sides of an experience. Look at the big picture. No experience is all good or all bad. Examine what is good about the bad parts. See how the energies work together to form a whole. Understanding the whole allows you to lose the good versus bad categories. It is all part of the same whole, and while some experiences are uncomfortable, great growth is possible as a result of the challenge. All parts of a story need to inform your decisions as you move ahead.

Your total experience determines whether adjustments may, or may not, be needed to your boundaries. Using the perspective of time, rethink past events that make up your old stories. Imagine the energies of the situation instead of just the raw emotion. What blessing happened as a result of your old story that would never have happened otherwise? What lessons did you learn? What strength did you acquire that you did not have before you were tested?

Cultivate open-heartedness. The essential impulse of creation is love. You are part of that impulse. You are the total of all your experience, emotion, and growth. Be willing to open your heart to others. Open your heart to you. Dare to actually say out loud, "I love you" without needing a response. Say it to yourself. Say it to others. Love because *you* love. Reciprocation feels nice to the ego but that isn't the important part. The love you give is the part that feeds your spirit. Share your heartfelt love without expectations. This will help create the generosity of spirit necessary to feel optimism.

Loving without expectation creates generosity of spirit. Generosity of spirit creates optimism. Realize it takes as much practice to become optimistic as you have given to being pessimistic, fatalistic, or resigned. Optimism isn't the old pie in the sky, wishful thinking, or rose-colored glasses glued to the bridge of your nose. It is an honest expectation that things will work out for the best. Remember the power of your thoughts. Hopefully you have begun changing your thoughts, your self-talk, and opinions to reflect what you really want instead of allowing outdated beliefs to reinforce the myths you have established. Positive restructuring of thought reinforces optimism. Optimism helps to optimize your reality.

Embrace the Fool. You have the ability to exert influence over your life. It is your right to do so but please don't take it so seriously! That will give you ulcers! Play every day. Foster an attitude of fun; be silly. Find the humor in every situation and use it to lighten your heart. The archetypal fool is the only one who can tell the truth to the king and keep his head because a fool makes the truth funny. Use the strategy of the fool and laugh every chance you get, teach others to laugh with you. The humility it takes to laugh at yourself is a blessing to your world and takes nothing away. Laughter is essential to perspective and a vaccine to boost your healthy boundaries. Laugh at yourself easily and also, laugh at life without recrimination or abusive intent. This will enhance your spirit and your boundaries.

Finally, take it easy on yourself. You are not built to do everything. When it becomes obvious that you are capable, whether on the job, at home, or in the community, people will try to get you to take on their projects and help with their problems. As word spreads, more people will come. Usually you feel obliged to agree. You are flattered or made to feel like you are the only one that can do the job. Alternatively, you are threatened or made to feel guilty if you don't comply with their demands. It is easy to overbook yourself. It is easy to become overloaded with demands from others. Be certain your calendar reflects a reasonable number of tasks and only ones that are valuable to you and your journey. Remember, you must respect your boundaries if anyone else is to do so.

Learn to say, "No." Many of the tasks you are asked to do are pieces of someone else's agenda. They don't further your goals, they don't give you pleasure; they don't add value to your life. It is possible, even at work, to say "no" without negative repercussions. Try saying, "I would love to commit to this project. Which of these other things do you want me to put on the back burner so I can do this one?" You have only so much time. Usually these extra tasks will still get done, just not by you. You will still be liked, and better yet, once the surprise settles down, you will be respected.

Saying "no" to other people's projects allows you to focus on what is uniquely yours. It gives you free time to think about where you are going and what you want to do. It allows you to establish goals and create that which is important for your own journey, for your own purposes. This is the greatest gift of heart you can give. The world needs people who are fulfilled and dedicated to doing a few things beautifully rather than struggling to do many things poorly.

Live life beautifully by doing what is important to you. Life is meant to be lived in joy. That is why happiness is the motivation behind your actions. Joy is the heart fire that will reacquaint you with the divine in yourself or burn you out if not reasonably contained. Boundaries, which keep out the distractions and clamoring of the world, give you time to think, pray, find, and build your dreams.

Questions for Your Journal

- What are my boundaries? Are they clear and active, or are they vague and unenforced with no substance?
- Boundaries - Pushing them to Violation: Remember one or two instances where my boundaries were clearly violated. What happened? What was the boundary? How do I feel about the emotional repercussions that followed? How did I allow this boundary to be violated?
- How did the four survival archetypes (child, victim, prostitute, and saboteur) manifest in these instances? Where else have they played a role in my life?
- Boundaries - Honoring them as Guardians: In what instances have I succeeded in protecting and honoring my boundaries? What motivated me in these instances? How did I feel before and after? How did honoring my boundaries change the stresses involved?
- How would I be perceived if I always had strong clear boundaries? How would boundaries change things?
- How can I create healthy boundaries?
- Who stops me? Whom do I stop?

Chapter 7

Fifth Word – Compassion

"It is lack of love for ourselves that inhibits our compassion toward others. If we make friends with ourselves, then there is no obstacle to opening our hearts and minds to others."

Unknown

Extreme Emotion: Anger

TCM Element: Wood Element

TCM Organ Systems/Meridians: Liver/Gall Bladder

Archetypes: Warrior, Guardian of Peace

Visionary, Guardian of Transcendence and Insight

Anger is so big! Anger is forbidden. It is destructive, evil, abhorrent, and dangerous! So much harm is done with anger. Anger never solves anything. Ladies do not get angry. How many of these statements align with your own feelings about anger? Anger can be big and explosive but, like all of the other extreme emotions, it is not good or bad. It is a tool. Feeling anger is the way you discover that something is wrong and needs to be addressed. Anger is one of the most dramatic of the warning bells in your tool box and is the perfect tool for clearing the air. Misused anger can be harsh and destructive but it is possible to direct and refine it with compassion. One thing is certain, anger can change things. It can create movement where previously there was stagnation and frustration. When the impediments to progress are exposed, something new can be created.

Anger can be terrifying. For many years I would just shut down if someone yelled at me in what I thought was anger. My brain would turn off and I was incapable of uttering a word or even moving. This kind of paralysis is a testament to the power of anger, and a clear sign that anger without compassion can be overwhelming.

Literally, compassion means, "to suffer together." Some people take it to the extreme and feel they must suffer as much as the person who is actually burdened. That is hardly the point of compassion, however. Compassion is to be motivated to help someone when you see them suffering. This does not infer that you rescue them, but that you hold space for their healing. Holding space is a practice of being fully present with someone who is struggling. There is no direction, judgment, or control on your part in regards to their process. You recognize their struggle is part of their journey and you are there exclusively to witness and support, no matter where the journey goes.

Let's explore compassion with the following exercise. Go slowly. Close your eyes and experience each part of the exercise. If possible, have someone read to you or go to my website, www. mkatherinemitchell.com/, where I will lead you through this experience. For purposes of flow during this meditation, I will use the words *them* or *they* to recognize that your choice in each section may be either male or female.

Sit comfortably.
Close your eyes. Take a deep cleansing breath.
Feel the room get quiet as you settle into position.

Feel your body relax. Notice how you are supported. Your feet are supported by the floor. The chair supports your thighs and back. Feel your shoulders relax; allow the tension in them to fall away. Your arms grow heavy as they lay quietly in your lap. Breathing is effortless. Air flows freely, easily into your lungs. Hear the quiet behind your eyes. Allow your mind to settle. Stray thoughts may come. Allow them to pass. Breathe deeply.

Now, take a few moments to call to mind the image of someone you love, someone who makes your heart feel light and happy. Feel the warmth of your love for this person as it fills your heart. Notice how effortlessly it extends to them through space. You know their fears. You can see where they feel vulnerable, uncertain. You know they want to be loved and appreciated. Watch as your love effortlessly surrounds them, supports them. Send your appreciation. Know that, like you, your loved one wants to live a life full of wonder and joy; to live a full and blessed life. You know their hopes and dreams. What do they wish for, for themselves? Wish them those things. What difficulties do they face? What story from their past haunts them now? Feel your compassion for their struggle, for their heartache. Send them loving kindness. See them surpass their obstacles and succeed. See them healed and happy. Send them gratitude and loving kindness. Feel the light this love brings to your life. Wish them well.

Breathe.

Now, think of someone you are acquainted with but do not know well. See that they have dreams, hopes. See their struggles and secret

87

wishes. Recognize the part of you that you see in them. Recognize that, just like you, they want to be loved, they want to be cherished. See how they want to feel appreciated. Send them your love. Send them appreciation. Know that they want to live a life of wonder and joy. They want to have a full and blessed life. Wish that their dreams come true. Feel compassion for them in their life, for their struggles, for their fears. You know they have fears. They are as you. Wish them well. Send them loving kindness. Feel happiness grow in your heart as you see them succeeding. Feel the gratitude you have for them as part of your life. Send them your love.

And breathe.

Now imagine someone with whom you feel uncomfortable. See an image this person. Take a slow breath. Allow the image to settle on your heart. Notice how this person is like you. Notice how they too are struggling with something in life. Perhaps they are troubled; it may be they had a difficult childhood. Notice that, just like you, they are doing the best they can. Send them loving kindness. Imagine their hopes and dreams. Listen for the quiet prayers of their heart. Understand that they want to be loved. They want to be respected; they want to be appreciated; to have a full life. Send them understanding and loving kindness. Like you, they are doing the best that they can. Wish them well. Wish them success. Feel compassion for them grow. Send them gratitude for the understanding they have given you. Thank them for the lessons they have helped you learn. Send them your love.

And Breathe.

Now, think of someone you don't like. Sit quietly with this image. Allow it to settle in a space in your heart.

Breathe.

Allow yourself to see that they have hopes and dreams and quiet prayers in their heart. Imagine how this person would look when unguarded, vulnerable. See that they are vulnerable; they want love; they want to be heard. Maybe, at some point, they have felt rejected, misjudged, and maybe humiliated. They may have been abused or neglected. They could even now, feel hurt, lonely, abandoned, or fearful. They may be ill. See, they are not so different from you. Just like you, they are doing the best they can with what they know right now. They want to be respected and appreciated. They want to be accepted. Just like you, they want to matter. Recognize they have dreams. Imagine what they hope for themselves. They want to live a full and blessed life. Feel your compassion and understanding expand. Feel your gratitude for them grow. They are part of the landscape of your life. They teach you and feed you the wisdom of their life just by being. Wish them well. Wish them peace. Wish them success. Wish them their dreams come true. Send them loving kindness.

Breathe.

And now, bring to mind an image of yourself. Breathe. Allow your own image to settle in your heart. Let judgment fall away. Let criticism fall away. Allow yourself to gaze on your image with kindness. With loving kindness and compassion watch the story of your life pass softly through your mind. Notice your triumphs and your struggles. See how you are doing the absolute best that you can. Smile gently at the tender part of yourself that feels misjudged, hurt, lonely, abandoned, or fearful. Call to mind your hopes and dreams. Listen to the quiet prayers of your heart. See how you want to feel loved; you want to feel cherished and appreciated. You want to live a full life, a life of wonder and joy. Send yourself love, send appreciation, send gratitude. Feel the wonder and joy of this love and this appreciation. Acknowledge the greatness and strength of your heart. Witness your happiness and success. Watch all your dreams come true. Send loving kindness. Send compassion.

Now, take a deep, slow, cleansing breath. Take some time. Come back slowly from this experience.

Did your compassion collapse when you were asked to imagine yourself? Sadly, this is often the case. You reject the most important person in your life and judge yourself unworthy of your own good will! This is a myth. In fact, this is one of the most common of the myths: I am not worthy. The honest truth is, you are worthy of regard and respect. You are most definitely worthy of your own regard and respect; you need it to make your journey.

Compassion for one's self is critical; yet it seems impossible to manage. You want to be comforted and supported, loved and accepted like anyone else. You want to be important. You want to be treated with kindness. You fear judgment from others, yet judge yourself more harshly than anyone else ever would. Frustrations and jealousy fester until it flames into anger and then, quite often, turns inward to create depression. You fear to act. You haven't realized that the source of the support and love you are missing is best found in yourself. This is where you must not fail: in your compassion for yourself.

Humans are not created to suffer; suffering is entirely optional.

You create suffering by misunderstanding the role people play in your life, and the role you play in theirs. If you remembered your soul contracts, you would know that you decided to have certain experiences in order to achieve specific goals for your soul growth. It is said that the people who love you the most on a soul level, by agreement, are the ones that give you your hardest lessons. These people are your greatest gifts.

We need to add to our definition. While compassion causes you to feel motivated to help someone when you see them suffering, it is not about being co-dependent. In reality an, "Oh, let me take care of you," or, "I will fix it for you," attitude is *dis*empowering. Compassion is being willing to do what is necessary to assist someone in taking their next higher step. You cannot take the step for them. Compassion occasionally means providing a wake-up call or a reality check. It also means loving them for who they are including the parts of them that are awake to the world of spirit and soul growth, as well as the parts of them that are still asleep or hiding. It's time to realize that true compassion is about honest support. It's time to put away the judge, jury, and executioner and love the whole of each person warts and all.

* * *

Once you are born you cannot remember what was taken into consideration when making your contracts and planning your lessons for this life. You do know, with great clarity, all of the details and ramifications and possibilities in your contracts *while* you are making them. I guarantee you, in my life in Africa, the woman who watched slavers destroy everything and everyone in her life did not feel compassion. It is true that finding compassion under some conditions will not be as simple as shuffling few thoughts. I can also say that I cannot imagine what would lead me to agree to that experience. As much as my heart ached, the truth is, I made a sacred contract with the slavers, my community, my husband, and my baby to have that experience.

Suffice it to say, if you are responding in anger, life is giving you an opportunity to learn or express compassion. This compassion is not for others, but for the part of you that you see in them. From this distance of many lives, I understand that the slavers were trying to make a living, possibly trying support a family. That slaver is not so much different than me after all. What would I do to earn money for my family? What would I do to survive? I would not choose murder and conscription now but it is a different time.

We all have our own stories. While you are not your story, walking this journey you call life feels very real, up close, and personal. In the quest for a perfect life mistakes are made. We hurt each other; you hurt yourself. This is not the intention, but it is often the outcome. Realize that, while you know more of your story than anyone, even you don't remember your whole story. Cut yourself some slack. Who but you can better appreciate the history and the complexities of your daily life? Who is better equipped to know exactly how to give you support, love, acceptance, and compassion than you are?

Life in the Shadows

Your shadow side is the part of you that you don't want to admit to having; yet it exists in all of us. Don't be afraid to look. There is no shame in having a shadow side. Each shadow is a blessing and a lesson plan. Besides, you cannot address something you don't realize is there. Once you understand your shadows, they can become great strengths and allies. Shadows are a source of potential empathy, understanding, and ultimately, compassion.

It is difficult to see your shadow side. Observe your reactions to daily life to discover it. You want to believe that you are good. That fact often puts blinders on your ability to recognize your shadow energies except as a reflection from someone else. Psychology calls this projection. You see and judge in others what you cannot bear to acknowledge in yourself. For example, a man who is appalled by watching a heavy person eat is, perhaps, feeling unworthy of being nourished himself. Perhaps he feels guilty about nourishing himself at some level. Maybe his disgust is a reflection of his own poor self-image. Since he is not consciously aware of his own eating issues (or self-approval issues), he condemns the person he sees eating. The people around you act as mirrors. What you judge in them is likely an issue, in some form, for you. It is important to step back and consider the possibility that a judgement of someone else has more to do with what you need to understand and address about yourself. In other words, it is less about them and more about you.

Compassion for one's self is the cornerstone of true compassion for others. Once you begin to feel compassion for your struggle and for your own shadows, you can grasp that you are doing the best you can in your situation with the understanding you have. This is not an excuse or justification. It is a deep understanding that allows you to dismiss your personal judge and look beyond self-castigation for what you can do better. It also allows you to extend that compassion to others.

You can begin to grow beyond your struggle by owning your story, not being owned by it. As long as you carry your personal tragedy or experience as baggage your story owns you. As long as you choose to suffer rather than take responsibility for the lessons you decided upon, your story owns you. To grow beyond your story you must honor opportunities you have created to foster growth and learn the lessons. Most importantly, you must view yourself with compassion rather than condemnation, contempt, or doubt. Again, when you can show yourself compassion, you will able to show true compassion for others.

Compassion comes from a level of humility created by the awareness that we are all walking a journey of spirit. We are spiritual beings having a physical experience. We are all doing the best we can with what we understand at this exact moment. The ability to do your best varies with illness, with fatigue and many other factors, but understanding the journey itself is a lifeline. It allows you to feel compassion and find a desire to help others from a level of understanding rather than superiority. Your compassion is your connection to spirit.

Compassion is not passive

Does having compassion mean you are supposed to sit by and let others bully you, enslave you, or persecute you because they are just trying to do what they believe will make them happy? No! Some lessons require that you fight, that you stand up for yourself from a place of love and respect for the needs of both your soul and theirs.

Sometimes the right thing to do is fight to promote the enlightenment of yourself and those with whom you have conflict. Krishna demonstrated this to Arjuna before the great battle in the Baghavad Gita. In this battle, Arjuna's army was arrayed against his father, brothers, and many of the people Arjuna loved. He was agonized and conflicted because of his great love for them. Krishna showed Arjuna how stopping his loved ones from pursuing their current path would be in the best interest of their soul growth and, therefore, the most loving and compassionate thing he could do. Of course, you don't have a God beside you giving advice, but you have God within you. Compassion is a gift.

Grief as great as I felt after the loss of my African family showed up again in another lifetime as compassion for the enslaved. This time I was a southerner. I left my family, much to their dismay, and joined the union army to fight in the Civil War. The part of me that felt cursed for not effectively fighting the slavers finally stood up against slavery. It is possible that, had I not done so, I would not have been able to consider the possibility that they were like me nor could I have found compassion for the slavers.

Compassion, empowerment, commitment, boundaries and choice are the tools you need to pick up so you can go forward through life. Choose empowerment over meekness. Commit to the greater good and set healthy boundaries with compassion.

Wood Element

(Liver and Gall Bladder)

"The mysterious powers of spring create wind in heaven and they create wood upon earth. Within the body they create muscles and of the five viscera they create the Liver. Of the colors they create the green color...and they give to the human voice the ability to form a shouting sound. In times of excitement and change they grant the capacity for control. Of the orifices they create the eyes, of the flavors they create the sour flavor, of the emotions they create anger."

Nei Ching

The wood element is associated with the liver (yin) and gall bladder (yang) organs and meridians. The sense organ is the eyes, the tissue is tendons. TCM suggests that when problems occur in these physical areas, taking a good look at anger and the associated emotions will help determine where to begin on your healing journey. Wood element's primal emotion is anger, with irritation, jealousy, frustration, and resentment being familiar offshoots. Your reaction to them runs the gamut from extreme defensiveness and hostility to insecurity. Physical symptoms may include migraines, heartburn, back pain or stiffness, fatigue, or eye problems. The color for the wood element is green, the tone is *shu*, the sense is sight, and the sound is shouting. Using these facts about the element during healing will help to release and soothe the intensity of the primal emotion of anger and will aid balance and growth.

The season of the wood element is spring with birth its associated developmental stage. It may be helpful to realize that anger is good at clearing away the debris of life so that new beginnings might occur, that is, the birth of new things. This is much like the new green shoots of spring coming up through the debris of winter and using the old and worn to enrich new growth. As it cleans up, it creates.

Remember, primal or extreme emotions are alarms. They signal that something is wrong and needs attention now! Also remember, emotions are just energy. None of your emotions are bad or evil. They just are. You get into trouble when you act on emotions inappropriately or when you hold on to them or try to bury them. How you express emotion determines how your life develops. To the ancient Chinese, strong emotions were perceived as impermanent but needing expression. Emotions are gifts that show you where your *re*actions need to be consciously chosen action. With time, these consciously chosen actions will become automatic responses.

Because you repeat experiences until you actually learn your lessons, you tend to create a habitual response. If dealing with anger is part of the lesson, you find you get angry more easily, more quickly, and you hold it longer. This is not a great cruel fate; it is a testament to how much you want to learn your lessons. Overcoming your shadow requires repeating experiences until the lesson is learned. The goal is remembering the *light* that you are.

As you saw with the meditation earlier in this chapter, compassion is the key to understanding that we all contain both light and shadow. With understanding comes the ability to balance emotions and make life-supporting choices. Yes, there will still be anger; it is sometimes an important tool, but it doesn't have to be a senseless, destructive, all-consuming fire!

Compassion extends the hand of hope. Any adult who has forgotten how to play or who has lost his or her smile certainly needs the tender regard of compassion. The man stuck in his wounds, or me in the past wrapped in anger and self-hate (victim), the woman trapped into doing too much work for hope of praise or promotion (prostitute), and the man convinced he cannot begin a new project or seek a partner because he is not good enough (saboteur) all need compassion. All need hope.

Wood Element Archetypes

WARRIOR: Guardian of Peace
VISIONARY: Guardian of Transcendence and Insight

Wood element archetypes are as specific to developing compassion as they are to the expression of anger. The basic archetypal energies for the wood element are warrior and visionary. Understanding the scope of these archetypes will help define the energies and impulses the wood element brings into your life.

Traditionally you think of the warrior archetype as a stoic, self-sacrificing hero who has great defensive skill, strength, and discipline. As a guardian of peace this archetypal energy transforms, slays if you will, judgments or criticisms from any source that would compromise your personal integrity. This is a warrior who knows when it is appropriate to fight. He or she knows what is worth fighting for. A challenged or shadow warrior would be like the slavers, more inclined to want victory at any cost, not caring about the suffering they caused. Their only care is for personal reward. This makes them shadow warriors or mercenaries. A shadow warrior is not a romantic energy, no knight in shining armor.

The warrior reflects the struggle to overcome your myths through acts of courage and compassion. The impulse may start with anger, a noticing of wrongs you do yourself encouraged by your self-induced limitations. In shamanism the warrior is that part of yourself willing to turn in myths and limitations for expansion and soul growth. Your personal warrior wants to be the hero of your own life story.

Visionaries have the ability to rise above, to see what others cannot, and to imagine what is possible. Visionaries dream of greater possibilities. The shadow visionary is willing to sell out to the highest bidder or perhaps alter his or her visions to make them more acceptable or profitable. This is prostitution of the visionary energies.

My son-in-law, Michael, expresses both visionary and warrior archetypes. He wrote, "I know, at every level of my being, that I am divine through my connection and outgrowth from God. And that is love, compassion, and in-joyment. Therefore, I get very aggressive when those [the ability to express or feel love, compassion, and being in joy] are minimized in any way." He remembers envisioning better things for slaves in ancient Egypt, rising up against slave masters. Michael stated, "I can tap into that rage/urge very easily. In this example, I was the one telling others that we could topple the masters; that we could fight our way to freedom, that I would take the first blows as we challenged our captors." Michael was able to envision a way forward out of bondage and, expressing the warrior archetype, was willing to lead the fight for freedom for his people.

Hopefully, you no longer must come to blows to settle disputes. Hopefully you know anger is better released at the gym or by other active means. Still there are people in bondage; there are bullies. Anger can fuel the ability to stand up to a bully which is the act of compassion spoken of earlier. You also see people who believe using violence is the only way they will be heard. Who is to say if these people are fueled by righteous indignation or by their shadow? Your judgement of the situation may show your shadow. It is certainly possible that participating in a cause could lead people to freedom or, it could be tantamount to entering the victim triangle. As far as you are able, you must send compassion and loving kindness to the people involved in violence in our world community. Compassion and loving kindness will support the people involved in a cause that is fair and just and will inspire healing in the rest.

What Can I Do?

Practice *self-care* as described in the Chapter 8 where the basic care you need is covered. Since we are often remiss in self-care it has been recommended after every section of the *Five Words*.

Reinforce your connection to Mother Earth. Walk in nature. Drink in a view of the beautiful green of her forests and fields with your eyes. Allow the sight to cool your anger and frustration.

Breathe in the color of deep forest green and exhale jealousy, irritability, frustration, and hurt. Use the sound "shu" during breathing exercises. Breathe in green, exhale "shu" to aid release of emotions. Dress in green. Paint your favorite room a beautiful green to temper emotions that can be so flammable. Surround yourself with wood and the beautiful things of spring.

There are many techniques for transforming from an anger-driven life to a compassion-led life. Learning to forgive is critical to this. The compassion meditation revealed that everyone is doing the best they can; each is working toward that which they believe will make them happy. We all have the same motivation.

Yet you get hurt and angry. This is where forgiveness comes in. Forgiveness isn't condoning behaviors. It doesn't mean that you swallow your emotions. To truly forgive and grow you must admit the caustic event really happened and that you are upset. Denial doesn't work. It is also important to accept and admit responsibility for your part in the events. Do not try to justify or rationalize. What were your perceptions, judgments, and reactions at the time? What are they now? Have compassion for yourself in this and extend that compassion to the person you feel harmed you. Realize that you need to accept others as they are and not as you want them to be; you cannot change or control them, you can only change yourself.

> *"Holding onto anger is like drinking poison and waiting*
> *for the other person to die."*
> Unknown

Forgiveness is for you. Your thoughts and awareness have energy that is tied to the quality of the emotions you are experiencing. Energies of anger and resentment are toxic when held and rehearsed, while energies of compassion and forgiveness heal and refresh. Every time you find yourself dwelling on events that caused you anger or resentment, your awareness and energy is directed into the past. It does no good there. It does, however, feed and strengthen the energy concentrated around the offense and allows it to have a greater impact on your health and happiness in this current time. Forgiveness is not for the other person, though it is a great gift to them. Forgiveness is for you.

Whenever you become aware that you are thinking angry and hurtful thoughts about the person you need to forgive, say a prayer of forgiveness and then bless them for helping you to learn about yourself and heal. Do this every time you find yourself thinking about the situation or person and then go on with your life. You can say, "I forgive ___(name)___ for all past deeds, thoughts and words. I release both of us. We are free." Say this for others and for yourself as many times as is necessary to release the toxic energies that have built up.

Most importantly, you must forgive yourself. Forgive any and all transgressions you feel you may have committed. Forgive your part in events for which you need to forgive others. Also, remember to have compassion for yourself and forgive the transgressions you did not actually commit. For example, a rape victim often accepts the belief of others that she must have done something to cause or deserve such treatment.

Forgiveness informs compassion just as compassion endows forgiveness. Compassion for your own experience is important to help you realize that many of the myths you hold on to do not accurately reflect your true self. Compassion will help you find what is true. Forgive yourself. Hold yourself in the light of compassion. [8]

Master your thoughts. Don't let them run you through the

---

[8] Resources for more detailed information on forgiveness can be found on my suggested reading list.

well-worn path of misinformation supplied by your myths! Think carefully and honestly about the motivations for your thoughts. Try to discover the source of your self-judgment as well as your judgements of others. What are the myths running in your head? When you are filled with anger, frustration, guilt, shame, or other judgments, what do you hear? Who do you hear? It may or may not be your voice you hear, but you can bet the content has been reinforced in you by others or by your own misinterpretation.

How are you doing with control? When you feel out of control or over-controlled, the experience gives rise to anger and/or resentment. Being completely helpless to stop what was happening to my family in Africa so long ago left me with long-lasting control issues. I always felt others were controlling me and it was easy for me to feel resentment over it. You don't, however, need an old story to have control issues. Most people have plenty of reasons from the present.

For control issues:

- Sit down with a pen and paper and make a list of everywhere you feel out of control or over-controlled. No details. Making a list gives you the opportunity to itemize without rehashing the circumstances. Make it quick and matter of fact so you don't add energy to the past. List any given item only once; condense if there are many interconnected parts.
- Consider the list one item at a time.
- Decide who is really doing the controlling?
  - What is the relationship to the person controlling? Is it possible you are acting from the child archetype and allowing this person to dictate what happens to you?
  - Are there parts of the issue that *are* under your control?
  - Are there parts you are trying to control that are really not yours? Be realistic about this aspect. If it is not yours to control, give it up.

- Is the energy needed to fix the problem greater than it is really worth? In other words, will continuing to focus on this issue make a substantive positive difference for you? If not, let go of the need to control. Really, just let it go.

- What can you do to take over the areas that are yours to control? Don't spend hours pondering this; make it more of a quick brainstorming.

- Are you having the same experience again and again with different people? For example, every job you get ends up with you overworked and promises forgotten. Perhaps this means your lesson is to step up and take control. Do it!

- Are you the one that is over-controlling or trying to control things beyond what is appropriate? If so, allow others their part. Relax, relinquish control.

- Consider carefully just what you need to control and where you need to let someone else to step up. Make it happen.

It is important to realize that being compassionate with yourself about your control issues will help them resolve because it will raise the possibility of a different path. Control issues consume huge amounts of energy. Let go, change your approach, delegate when you are holding too much, step up and act when you are not controlling what is yours.

Sometimes control issues are inextricably tied up with depression. If your anger has turned inward and is manifesting as depression, you are probably tired, lethargic, and unmotivated. Despair haunts you. You feel you have no control and no choices. Be assured, if this is true, you have bought into the victim archetype.

Actually, you are making choices all of the time. Now it is time to choose to change your situation. It can be very difficult to pull yourself out of the quagmire depression brings. Sometimes just getting some exercise will do it. Otherwise, begin by doing the following:

- Be gentle with yourself, especially if your depression comes from grief. Some things just need time.

- Quickly summarize your situation. A list format is helpful since the summary is not meant to add negative energy to your situation.

- Do not judge, justify, or castigate yourself. Take charge.

- Choose to silence the part of you that believes in *poor me*. As much as it is miserable, depression carries with it a chance to pull yourself into a better situation than you imagine.

- Decide what aspect of the list you would like to change and how to do it. Can you move? Can you go out to meet different people? Can you change your employment? When you are depressed it certainly feels impossible to muster this kind of *can do* but you must make a choice.

- Whatever it is that you would like to see change, give yourself permission to do it! The consequences of taking a chance are generally not as destructive as continuing with depression.

- Include the affirmation, "I am safe and supported in life." Repeat this every time you doubt that you can change your circumstance.

- If things are bad enough, find a counselor. Find a counselor who can help you step out of the victim archetype. You do not want someone to commiserate with, you need someone to help you empower yourself.

Use the Serenity Prayer which is widely used by groups such as Alcoholics Anonymous: "God grant me the serenity to accept the things I cannot change, courage to change the things I can, and wisdom to know the difference." It is short and easy to remember. Some things you need to control; other things you do not. The prayer is a gentle reminder.

Lessons are not necessarily easy to learn. You have attained a certain comfort level with how things are and it is much easier to complain than it is to act differently. It is easy to fall back on old habit patterns and myths by using sarcasm, rage, or jealousy. Backsliding is easy until you truly understand that you put challenges in your life plan because easier isn't necessarily better.

Every circumstance has some gift to give you. The ultimate gift is the ability to act with compassion in all situations as a first response. Other gifts may be courage to act, self-assertion, clarity, and so on. Each situation also has something to teach you: decisiveness, *response* ability, to step up and act, for example. It can be uncomfortable stretching beyond your habitual level of performance, but if you can find the gifts and the lessons inherent in your circumstances you will be able to see just how compassion fits into a more fulfilled you.

Ultimately, Compassion guides you. You do not intentionally get things wrong; you do not really hate yourself. In a corner of your heart your inner self is jumping up and down screaming for your love. In some quiet corner of your soul you know you are essentially divine in origin, however you define divine. You have sometimes been misled; sometimes you have unknowingly misconstrued messages and misled yourself. It is time to stretch these sore sorry myths and become flexible in your emotional body, just as in your physical body. Once you begin to believe in a compassionate story of your life, you can let go of anger, cynicism, impatience, resentment, judgments, and other negative stories about yourself. You can begin to infuse that essential love into your life.

Questions for Your Journal

Considering all the information about compassion, answer the following questions:

- Who is most in need of my compassion?
- To whom am I most resistant to extending compassion?
- Who is the most important person in my life?
- Where is my compassion for the most important person in my life?

- What blocks the flow of compassion and loving kindness in my relationships?
- What choices do I need to make in order to grow in loving kindness and compassion every day?
- With whom am I angry? Quickly make a list.
  - Where do I rank on this list?
  - When thinking about these people, what similarities do I see in me? Are they acting like a mirror to show me a part of myself I don't want to see? Take the example of a woman who is angry that her husband always keeps her waiting thus keeping her from her own projects. When she looks closer, however, she sees that many times she puts her own projects on hold by spending her time on social media. The husband wasting her time is a reflection of her own time wasting.
- How can I begin the process of forgiveness and compassion?
- How can I forgive and have compassion for me?

Please consider that *you* are the person most in need of compassion in your life. You are, more than likely, harder on you than anyone else.

Food for Thought

The Five Words takes you on the journey to wholeness. When working on compassion, the choice is to turn off the voice of the judge, jury, and executioner. Compassion comes from a choice to understand that we are all doing the best we can at any given moment. It is a choice to be kind or unkind. Forgiveness is a choice. Continuing to pursue and feed your wounds as if they define you and until they do so is a choice. Boundaries provide opportunity for choice constantly. Do you choose to be taken advantage of or do you choose to say, "No"? You get to choose where your boundaries are just as you choose to expect, and demand, that they are respected. You get to choose how to respond when boundaries are violated. You choose to fold or to fly! Whether you choose to make a commitment to yourself and act in your own behalf is one of the greatest choices you make. Without *boundaries, compassion, and commitment* there is no ground for *empowerment. Choice* determines all!

Chapter 8

Self-Care

"Why do you stay in prison
when the door is so wide open?"

Rumi

The body is the "buck stops here" part of the energy system. This means that your body will perfectly store the energy of any emotion, thought, or experience you do not address. Any of the extreme emotions or their associated emotions, will cause problems when their energy is not dealt with properly. If your approach to dealing with these uncomfortable emotions is to deny them or stuff them down, sooner or later your body will complain. If you recognize which extreme emotion you are having challenges with, you have a starting point. If you do not recognize the emotion, consult your body. Areas that tend to give you trouble clue you into which emotions you are likely dealing with and, possibly, what the big themes in your life lessons are. For example, my lungs direct me to the theme of unresolved grief and a task of finding hope and self-worth. Consult the chapters listed for more information on the following emotions:

EMOTIONS	CHAPTER	ASSOCIATIONS
Fear, loneliness, and insecurity	Three	Kidney/bladder meridians Bones and ears
Grief, despair, and shame	Four	Lung/large intestine meridians Skin and nose
Worry, suspicion, and self-doubt	Five	Spleen/stomach meridians Muscle/flesh and mouth
Shock, vulnerability, and excitement	Six	Heart/small intestine and Pericardium/triple burner meridians Vessels and tongue
Anger, depression, and resentment	Seven	Liver/gall bladder meridians Tendons and eyes

You need to be your first priority!

Make time to rest when you are tired. If you cannot nap, take five minutes to inhale slow deep breaths into your belly as you visualize energy coming into your crown. Soak in a tub with your choice of bath salts, bubbles, and candlelight. Read a book that isn't required reading for work or school. Use energy work sessions to help clear emotions and/or physical symptoms. These can include shaman, acupuncture, medical qigong, and reiki among others. Get massages, reflexology, or other therapies to comfort and relax you. It's okay and even advisable to indulge yourself when you need to rest and rejuvenate.

It is said, *crying cultures the heart.* Please, cry if you need to. Allow your tears to wash away resentment, envy, or fear. Allow them to clear long term feelings of guilt, shame, or powerlessness, *etc.*

Whatever it is, the tears won't last forever. Allowing your body to release the stored emotions will free you to stand in your power and act from your soul guided heart.

Use your body. Exercise will help you blow off steam when anger runs hot; it will ease the lethargy of depression; it will move energies stagnant from worry, and thaw energies frozen in fear. Exercise calms anxieties, gives time for perspective to develop, and generally feels better than being stuck.

You don't have to join a gym and work out for hours. Dance, walk, do qigong, or tai chi, but do so regularly. The prescription movements of medical qigong address specific organ meridians, emotions, and thereby, disease. It makes an excellent, gentle exercise program. Enjoy running, lifting weights, swimming, Zumba, or dance. Of course, exercise doesn't replace actually dealing with your issues. For some people, exercise can be an addiction or a way to escape facing problems. Used correctly, it is a way to calm or energize the system enough to ensure positive action is possible.

Work, but also play! Create a balance between your work life and your home life that allows your body to recharge and blow off steam. Find something you like to do: sing, paint, play tennis, racquet ball, or another favorite sport. Build models, make crafts, play a musical instrument, or pull out that favorite thing you did as a kid and do it again! Get off the couch! Video games can be quite fun but when they are played obsessively, they are the same as any other addiction. More than that, they can stimulate the fight/flight response in the body. Your body cannot tell the difference between the game and real threats and feelings of doom. Instead of screen time do something that feeds your soul.

Watch what you put in your mouth. Eat only healthy foods at regular intervals. Eat small meals more often to keep blood sugar stable. Avoid sugary, high-carbohydrate, low-nutrition foods. These foods are every bit as addictive as any other drug with the subsequent nervous system reactions. Do not use artificial sweeteners. Many foods are packaged with labels that claim great health benefits.

In general, if it is packaged, it is over processed and needs to be avoided. Choose real whole foods instead.

Meditate. Meditation has been studied extensively and has been shown to relieve hypertension and provide stress management. If meditation in the "find yourself" arena is too hokey for you, meditation for stress relief should get your attention. After all, who is free of stress? You might consider meditating about all the ramifications of a beautiful thought or poem. This type of meditation is contemplation meditation. Choose your own life supporting thought to meditate on. When troubling thoughts interfere, quietly put them aside and continue.

The best meditation does not have a theme however; it is more about finding that calm space in you that refreshes you and allows you to heal. It gives you an opportunity to silence the external and internal chatter and be with yourself. The type of meditation isn't as important as a dedication to practice. Transcendental Meditation is excellent but please don't choose your own mantra. Words are powerful and not all are life supporting. Mindfulness meditation is wonderful. Your own process is fine so long as it puts you in touch with your quiet center. This is that place in you that has been buried by the pressure of experience and the shout of myth.

Yoga is also a good way to connect body, mind, and spirit. There are many types of yoga for young and old. Choose one that fits your style and practice any postures and meditations that you can learn. Both will help balance you and connect you to what is essentially you.

Breathe. Breathing may seem pretty obvious. It is essential to life, but it is also essential to how you spend your life. Breathing varies. You hold your breath when afraid, breathe rapidly when angry, and your breath catches in joy and sadness. Its pace depends on emotion. Conscious breath work calms and clears the emotions.

Breathing techniques can be simple:

- Inhale so the belly rises before the chest recognizing how the diaphragm pulls air deep into the lungs. This will cause your breathing to be deep rather than shallow. Learning to breathe this way throughout the day will help all aspects of the body, mind, and spirit connection.

- Breathe deeply. Inhale through the nose and exhale through the mouth. Make an intention to heal, energize or soothe. Intend to gain understanding, clarity, calm, or whatever is appropriate. Imagine and feel that unconditional love is coming in with the inhale and that stress is leaving with the exhale.

- When doing long meditations with Transcendental Meditation we were taught breath work called pranayama. It calms the experience of stress release and allows energies to flow and deepen. Place your right thumb on the right nostril, inhale through the left. Use your middle finger to close the left nostril, remove your thumb and exhale through the right. Inhale through the right nostril and replace the thumb. Remove the finger from the left nostril and exhale. Inhale left, exhale right. Inhale right, exhale left. Continue the pattern for five to ten minutes or more. Consistent practice will help balance your energies.

- Trace the infinity sign (∞) with your finger on your hand. Breathe in as you take three seconds to draw the left circle of the infinity sign. Pause and hold your breath for one second at the center, then breathe out as you take three seconds to draw the right circle. Hold your breath again for one second and start over. Make this a fluid, relaxing movement: left circle for three, hold for one, right circle for three, and hold for one. With practice you will be able to draw the infinity sign and calm yourself without concentration on technique.

Make a breathing practice part of your meditation practice. They are very complimentary. There are many meditative, yogic, and shamanic traditions that teach breathing techniques besides those already mentioned here. Books and CDs are available on the subject or you can take classes. Learn breathing techniques to increase your connection to your true self, your inner quiet, and your soul.

Congested energies from stress and negative thought processes create stiffness, pain and disease in the body, but they also impact other energetic levels. Since your emotions are directly tied to your thoughts, it makes sense to practice mind mastery: take responsibility for, and control over, your thoughts.

Thoughts have power. Remember the muscle testing we did earlier in Chapter Two? Imagine that each thought you have is a little prayer arrow that goes straight to the heart of whomever you are thinking about. That is, in fact, what happens. Now, with that in mind, consider prayer arrows and your own self-talk. What does your self-talk sound like? How often do you tell yourself, "Oh, you idiot!", "You are so stupid!", or "You will never get it right!"? Sometimes the messages you give yourself are so mean-spirited they make these example statements look like praise. You curse yourself with messages inspired by your myths all day long, over and over. Like magic, they become self-fulfilling prophesies. If you say, "I'm so clumsy" often enough, you will be; your prayers are answered. Control your thoughts. Use your prayer arrows mindfully. Substitute affirmations for the mean-spirited self-talk you are working to change.

Affirmations do not replace action! That being said, affirmations, used properly, reprogram your brain and allow for different thoughts and beliefs. This is part of mind mastery. Affirmations are the truth you long for. They work because they are the actual truth, if only your negative affirmations were not in the way.

To construct a positive affirmation, "I never get anything right," could become, "I will get it right." This is a much better thought. Still, there is an inherent future time when 'getting it right' will happen. You really want affirmations constructed to reflect what is wanted *now*. "I will get it right," sounds good but is less powerful than, "I get it right." Create positive affirmations spoken in present tense.

It can be tricky to come up with the right affirmation. Your myths and associated habits don't go down without a fight. A good affirmation will often feel so untrue as to be laughable and you may be uncomfortable, maybe even embarrassed, speaking or even thinking it. That is a sure sign you are on the right track.

Once you have your affirmations, what do you do with them? The secret to getting an affirmation to reprogram your thought process is to repeat it hundreds of times a day, or more. Once or twice won't do much, especially at first while you don't believe it. You have said your negative affirmations sourced from your personal myths millions of times in your life. It will take at least as many positive affirmations to reprogram your mind. Create strong positive messages and repeat them incessantly, especially when you catch yourself repeating old negative statements.

Say affirmations out loud to the face you see in the mirror. Mirror work is very effective. The squirmier you feel about looking at yourself in the mirror and saying, "You are amazing and I love you," the more you need to do just that. This isn't about stroking the ego but about reaching the little person inside of you that really doesn't believe in his or her own worth. Put post-it notes everywhere you are likely to look to remind you what your new thoughts are. Practice them while driving in the car during your commute. If you must fake it till you make it at first, so be it!

Master your mind. Realize you dream your world into being with every thought, word, and deed. Affirm a thousand times a day what you want out of life in positive terms and let the rest go. Some commonly needed affirmations follow:

- I am safe
- I am worthy
- I am supported by the universe in all that I do
- I am the creative force in my life

Our society is plagued by an emphasis on the mind. Education is prized over intuition, success over process, and practicality over magic. While education, success, and practicality are not bad things, when they are the only things valued your life takes a turn for the dismal. Intuition is the voice of your soul. *Listen.* Process is the voice of your emotions. *Feel* your emotions, don't think about them. *Magic* is where the dream of life happens. Create your dreams!

Laugh. Laugh. Laugh. Lighten it up! Laughter really is the best medicine. It is possible to find story after story about people curing their cancer through laughter. What else might be cured with laughter? Life is meant to be lived in joy! Watch funny movies, play with happy people. Play the tummy game where you have a group of friends and each one lays their head on someone else's tummy around the room. Sooner or later, someone will start laughing and soon, everyone will be laughing. Play the fool. Find something funny in every situation. Laugh to stay sane; laugh just because you can; laugh when any other response plunges you into darkness. Laughter is a gift you can give yourself. It will take tension out of you. It will add light. Laugh!

Your body reflects all that is going on in your world. It is the mirror of your experience, emotions, and attitude. Emotions are there for a reason. If you actually experience them, learn from them, and release them you save yourself potential health problems. Since your body reflects emotions, you can find your ignored emotions by paying attention to how your body feels. Begin by scanning your body. What are the sensations? Are there any places that feel tight or painful, for example? Feel everything there is to feel about this tight and painful area and watch what happens to it as you quietly hold your attention on the sensation. How big is it? When you watch the sensation, does it get bigger or smaller? Does it move around? Try to magnify the sensation. Try to make it worse. This will be difficult because of the tendency to want to resist or suppress feelings. Do it anyway. Do whatever feels like you need to do next: if you need to cry, do so; if you need to scream, do that too. Whatever happens, just keep following the sensation. Watch how it changes and moves. Eventually it will subside and/or give you some insight.

You can even ask the body part that is hurting what it is trying to tell you. Stay out of your mind; this is a process of awareness, not thought. Listen for an answer with all of your senses. Do you smell something, see something, or hear a sound that could shed light on your experience. What are the associations you have with what you are sensing? How old do you feel as you experience this sensation? Do not downplay your senses or your imagination and their role in creating understanding. Just observe and stay out of your mind. Do not judge. Stay open to what happens and allow your experience to inform you. Get out of your way. It is a process.

If you are following the process and nothing seems to be changing, get up and move your body. Try to match the movement to what you are feeling. Demonstrate with your body what your feelings look like: dance, stomp, or fold into a ball. Do any physical movement that may help you to express the feeling. Do you need to spin, or pound a pillow, or roll on the floor? Gradually, when it feels appropriate, change any restrictive or harsh movement into a more flowing and free one. Movement changes the channel of your perception, so to speak, and often will bring insight where stillness and thinking cannot. As a cerebral society we don't often move with and through our emotions. That is why this technique works! Move until you find some release, relief, or insight no matter how silly you might feel. After the emotions have shifted, take some time to journal your impression and experience.

Throughout all of this, the mind needs to be an observer. Your archetypal judge needs to be put in the proverbial next room. These experiences are neither a competition nor a performance. They are a chance to actually listen as your body talks about what it needs, about what you need.

If you need help, get help. The proper counselor can work wonders. Interview prospective counselors to make sure they have the right attitude and a compatible philosophy. Use their services to move ahead if you are struggling. Having said that, remember you don't need to wait for someone else to fix you. Indeed, fixing you is your job! The fact is you are the only one who can do this work. Others can help with insight or encouragement but the work is yours to do. Empower yourself, fix yourself. Fixing yourself takes time and patience. You will find yourself working on things you thought were already healed. This is normal. Allow yourself as much time, patience, love, and compassion as it takes.

Chapter 9

Afterword

*"Love is the cure.
For your pain will keep giving birth to more pain
until your eyes constantly exhale love as effortlessly
as your body yields it's scent"*

Rumi

Healing is a journey. It is circuitous and repetitive. The same lesson will be repeated over and over, in different circumstances, different iterations. If you are doing your work and learning from these opportunities, each repetition of the lesson teaches something more refined. When you are not paying attention the lessons becomes harder and harder until finally, screaming in pain, you do pay attention. Again, this is not evil or devilish. You planned it this way to ensure you do what you intended for this life. You are rather like a chambered nautilus making your slow way into the larger reality by deliberate degrees. Each time you are presented with a lesson, you have an opportunity to refine your understanding, purify your commitment for right action, and climb one chamber closer to the fullness of yourself.

I will not lie to you. Finding your true path is hard. I have been on this journey consciously for as long as I can remember.

117

I have always been driven to find the path back to peace, to love. There were times when the urgency of this work drifted into the background as more physical matters took precedence. Even so, the need was there for me to find the way back. There were times when I was so far removed from my path I felt as though I stared into the pits of hell. This experience is known as the dark night of the soul. It sounds very dramatic. Let me just say, it is much more painful than dramatic.

Then there was a time when I thought I would experience exactly what I was looking for, unbounded, unconditional love, if only for a moment. I walked away from the experience crying and angry. I felt I had been minimized in some way. I held myself and my experience up to the stories of others and found myself cheated. What an error. The next morning, it just took a glance at the right image to trigger an understanding of the gift I had been given. I was flooded with love! I experienced unbounded, unconditional love and stood amazed and humbled.

Eventually, I learned how to journey in the way of the shaman and I went back into the life in Africa. This is my journal entry of the experience.

"I have been having coughing and shortness of breath for a very long time. Though I can't remember them, my dreams have frequently caused me to awaken with chest pain and racing pulse. I decided to take the shaman's journey to the source of the chest pain. I played a drum tape to help me attain the correct state and asked for a guide to take me to the source of my pain. None came. As I settled further into the process, I began to feel into my pain. I made a conscious effort to see how big it was, if it moved, and if it got worse or better with attention. At some point a black hole appeared in my awareness. It seemed like a heart valve but large, shiny, and blacker than black. I was meant to go there."

"At last my animal guide came for me and, together, we entered the black hole. It was so dark I could only follow him by faith. Finally, we came out amid trees. I saw no one. It was quiet. I became distantly aware of carnage. It registered on my psyche before I actually saw the wreckage of homes and people. Then I felt the madness, pure unadulterated insanity, and then, I found me. I was lying pierced between my heart and lung with a wooden shaft of some sort. I was alive. I saw the color of my beautiful skin, my shoulder and breast. I could not see my face nor could I, at first, reach the mind that had been my mind. It seemed like we fussed about the shaft a bit and I tried to calm and reassure. Finally I said, "I have her, she is safe. She is no longer taken, she is well." I repeated this message over and again until I watched hope mixed with mistrust take the place of panic and pain in the eyes that now looked to me. I was guided to do death rites for my former self. She and I so desperately needed to be allowed to pass through this horror. In time I begged her to come back with me. I told her she could talk to our child; she could hold our child."

At first I was uncertain if she understood. Then I was uncertain she came with me. That evening, however, my/our daughter called spontaneously. She was bright, and happy, and sweet to talk to. When it finally came time for bed I knew my former self had come home. It felt as if two giddy kids were chattering in my head. "Was that really her?" "Did you hear her?" "I told you she is wonderful." And so it went.

It is interesting that the entrance was "blacker than black." That is the color associated with the water element. It is the color you breathe in to build up the kidneys and ameliorate fear. Also, I followed my guide by faith, a most potent antidote to fear. Her grief was palpable and she struggle for air. Death rites soothed some of the grief, anger, and shock of the events that had transpired. She was able to hear my assurances and feel my compassion. Knowing I had our daughter empowered her enough to set aside her primal emotions and come with me.

At the time I decided to take this journey, I was already well into writing this book. As often happens, writing brought up much that I thought I had already addressed. As you now know lessons repeat until they are learned and healing takes place. As a result, by way of a healing crisis (my cough and chest pain), I was given the opportunity to do some further healing. For 2 days after the journey I was cough and pain free. Since then my symptoms have changed. Clearly, I have either more healing to do on this experience or something else is coming up for me to heal. Most importantly, I brought back a lost part of my soul that evening and she has since hugged and held her child.

Finding your true path is essential. Regardless of your thoughts about what comes after this life, if you want to leave a positive, lasting impression on the world when you die, you must do this work. Finding your true path is how you develop the full potential you were born with. Finding your true path allows you to touch the world in a manner that makes a difference to the people who come after you and not just your children. The entire world is made better by each person who follows their dream (plan) of being. In order to follow that dream you must:

- *Choose* to have faith instead of living in fear.
- Choose to *empower* yourself, instead of allowing others control of your destiny while you live in some manifestation of grief, despair, or regret.
- Choose to *commit* instead of being batted about by indecision, confusion, and worry.

- Choose to create your *boundaries* rather than allow others to use you and your resources until you are spent and become cold, indifferent, or anxious.
- Choose *compassion* for the most important person in your life. Hopefully by now you now know that person is you.

Thank you for taking this journey with me. I wish you blessings in your lessons and healing for your personal journey toward fullness of your soul's purpose.

In love always,
Katherine

Further Reading

Albert Ellis, Ph.D., and Robert A Harper, Ph.D. 1961. *A Guide to Rational Living*. Englewood Cliffs, N.J., Prentice-Hall.

Albert Ellis, Ph.D., *How to Stubbornly Refuse to Make Yourself Miserable About Anything Yes Anything!* 2006. New York, NY. Kensinton Pub.

Anodea Judith & Judith Vega. 1993. *Sevenfold journey: reclaiming mind, body & spirit through the chakras*. Freedom, CA. Crossing Press.

Barry Neil Kaufman. 1991. *Happiness Is a Choice*. New York. Fawcett Columbine.

Carolyn Myss. 2001. *Sacred contracts : awakening your divine potential*. New York. Harmony Books.

Charles, A. Moss, MD. 2010. *Power of the Five Elements: The Chinese Medicine Path to Healthy Aging and Stress Resistance*. Berkeley. North Atlantic Books.

Collin Tipping. 2009. *Radical forgiveness: a revolutionary five-stage process to heal relationships, let go of anger and blame, find peace in any situation*. Boulder, CO. Sounds True

Doreen Virtue. 1958. *Constant craving: what your food cravings mean and how to overcome them*. Carson, CA, Hay House.

Harriet Beinfield, L.Ac. and Efrem Korngold, L.Ac., O.M.D. 1992. *Between Heaven and Earth, A Guide to Chinese Medicine.* New York. Ballantine Books.

Louise L. Hay. 1987. *You can heal your life.* Santa Monica, CA. Hay House.

Luc Bodin, M.D., Nathalie Bodin Lamboy, and Jean Graciet ; translated by Jon E. Graham., 2016, *The book of ho'oponopono : the Hawaiian practice of forgiveness and healing.* Rochester, Vermont. Destiny Books.

Melody Beattie. 1992. *Codependent No More: How to Stop Controlling Others and Start Caring for Yourself.* Center City, MN. Hazelden

Professor Jerry Alan Johnson, Ph.D., D.T.C.M., D.M.Q. 2002. *Chinese Medical Qigong Therapy.* (China) (5 Volumes). Pacific Grove, CA. International Institute of Medical Qigong.

About the Author

Fifty years ago Katherine Mitchell took her first formal steps toward healing and spiritual growth. It began with meditation. Two years later she left for Spain and a six month intensive training course in meditation practice and teaching. She maintained her practice of meditation through school, marriage, and child rearing. Inspired by the desire to heal and continue her search for soul growth, Katherine went through Reiki training and, in time, became a Reiki master. She studied with the Pennsylvania School of Spiritual Healing and graduated from both their energy healing and intuitive programs. It was there she studied archetypes and the work of Carolyn Myss. Katherine has also studied acupressure which led her to medical qigong. Ultimately she completed master level training at the East Coast Institute of Medical QiGong (formerly International Institute of Medical QiGong). In keeping with her love for earth based energy medicine, Katherine has spent the past several years studying with Gateway School of Shamanism. She is an ordained a minister through the Sanctuary of the Beloved. Her ministry is represented in her healing practice and through *the FIVE WORDS*. She brings all of these tools to her private sessions. She also enjoys sharing her knowledge through lectures and workshops.

Currently Katherine lives in Pennsylvania with her husband and assorted critters. She has three amazing daughters and seven grandchildren unless you count daughters from other mothers and their children.

www.mkatherinemitchell.com
innerheart4healing@gmail.com

Made in the USA
Lexington, KY
11 October 2018